GOLF FEVER

TEE OFF TIME
OVER 100 LAUGHS

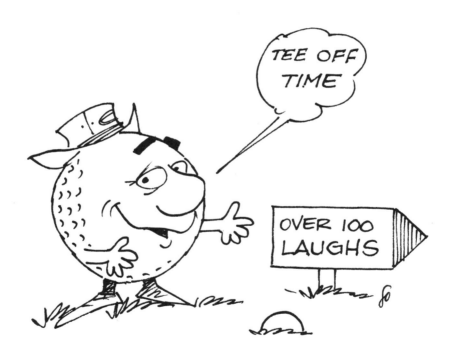

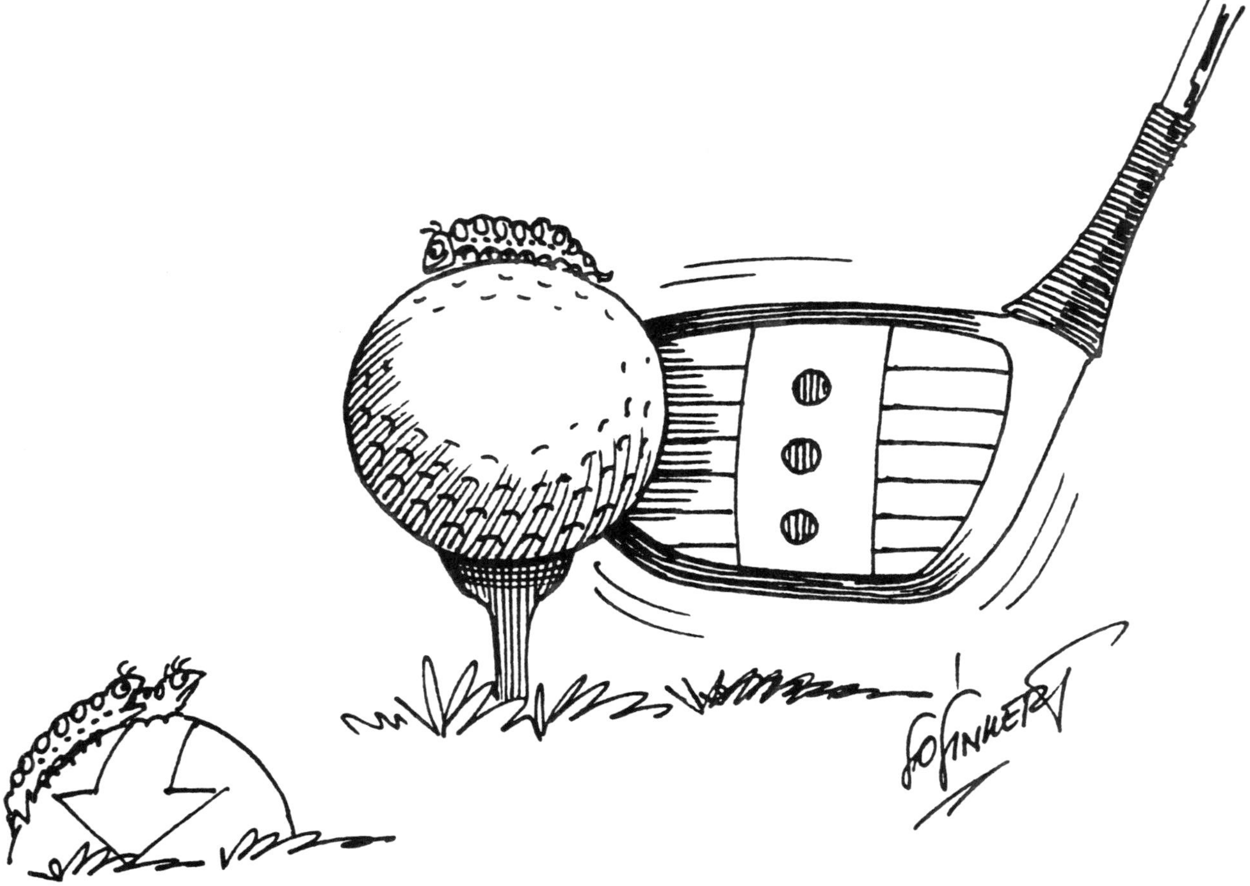

" I CERTAINLY HOPE HE TOOK OUT FLIGHT INSURANCE."

GOLF FEVER

by

Lo Linkert

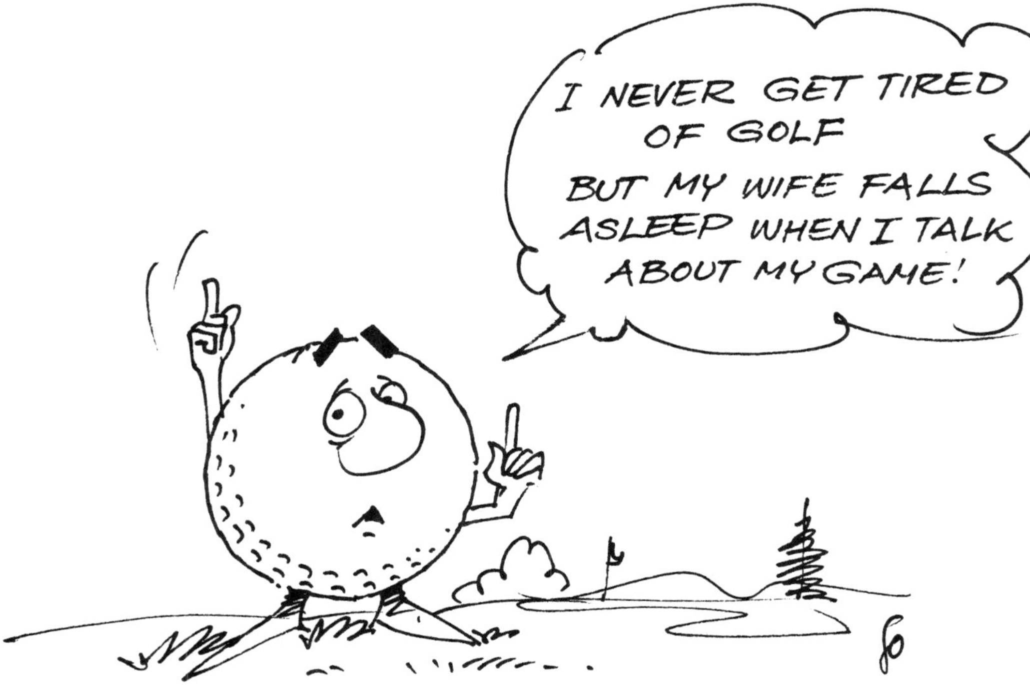
I NEVER GET TIRED OF GOLF
BUT MY WIFE FALLS ASLEEP WHEN I TALK ABOUT MY GAME!

SPECTACLE LANE PRESS

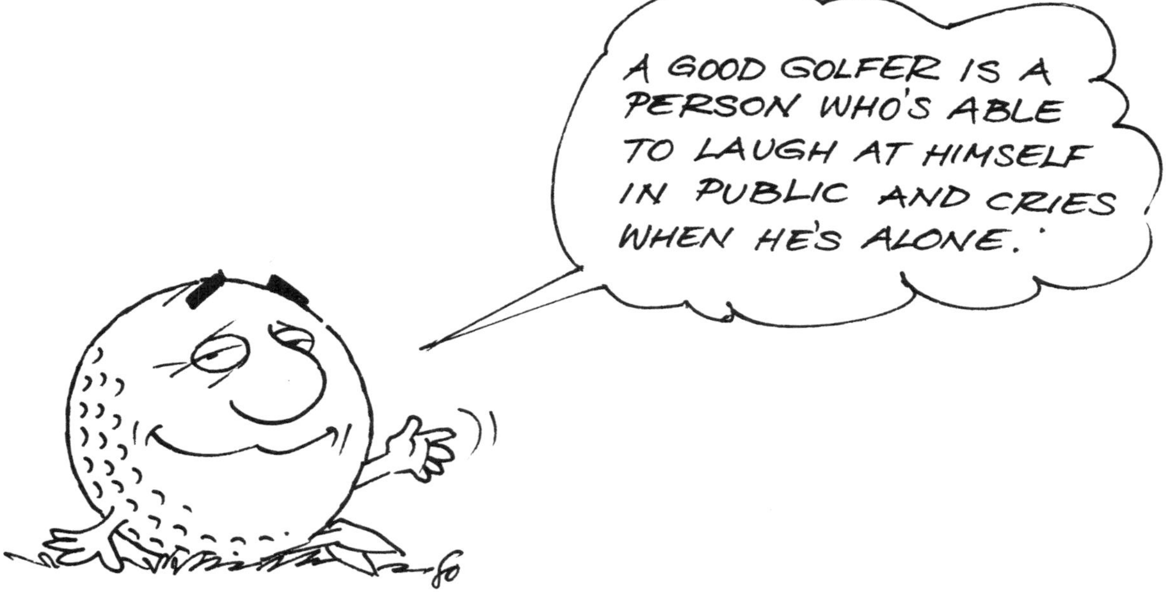
A GOOD GOLFER IS A PERSON WHO'S ABLE TO LAUGH AT HIMSELF IN PUBLIC AND CRIES WHEN HE'S ALONE.

Published by Spectacle Lane Press
Box 34, Georgetown, CT 06829.

ISBN 0-930753-16-X

Published simultaneously in the United States and Canada.
Printed in the United States of America.

FOREWORD

This book is dedicated to my three golfing darlings: my wife Inge, my daughter Colleen and my granddaughter Morgan Leigh.

I feel a certain responsibility to them when it comes to golf because I introduced them to the game. There have been times they loved me for it. Other times they didn't love me that much, especially since, as I did, they caught golf fever and have been unable to get rid of it, even when things, as they often do, have not gone too well.

I have had golf fever for over 30 years. As every golfer knows, the golf bug gets under your skin and gives you a life-long itch, which goes up and down with your handicap, but never leaves you.

Golf fever is contagious, as my wife, daughter and granddaughter have found out. They have also found out that with the injection of a little success (even one good shot at the 18th hole) and of a little humor, it becomes a pleasant itch that makes life in general more bearable.

I have done my best to provide ample injections of humor through my golf cartoons and golf books, not only for my family, but for golfers and golf fans around the world.

Golf Fever is my twelfth golf cartoon book, and, like my eleven others, it is intended to provide a humor treatment that will ease whatever pains might come with golf fever while greatly enhancing the experiences that make the wonderful game of golf one of the most maddening, yet rewarding and enjoyable, of diseases.

LO LINKERT

GOLF WAS FUN TIL I READ THE RULEBOOK!

IN GOLF YOU CAN'T WIN... WHAT YOU'RE GAINING FROM EXERCISE YOU'RE LOSING IN EGO!

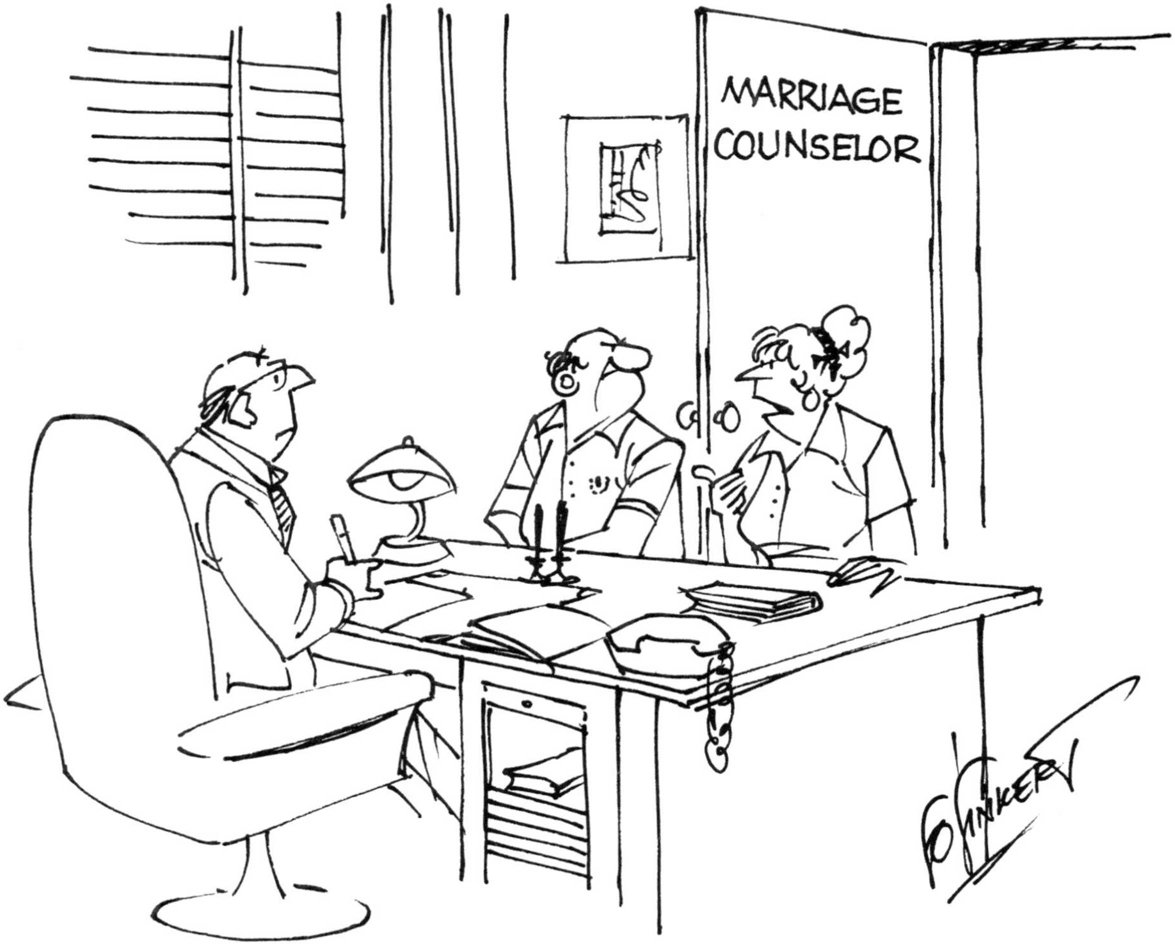
MARRIAGE
COUNSELOR

"OUR MARRIAGE WAS PERFECT UNTIL MY HANDICAP BECAME LOWER THAN HIS."

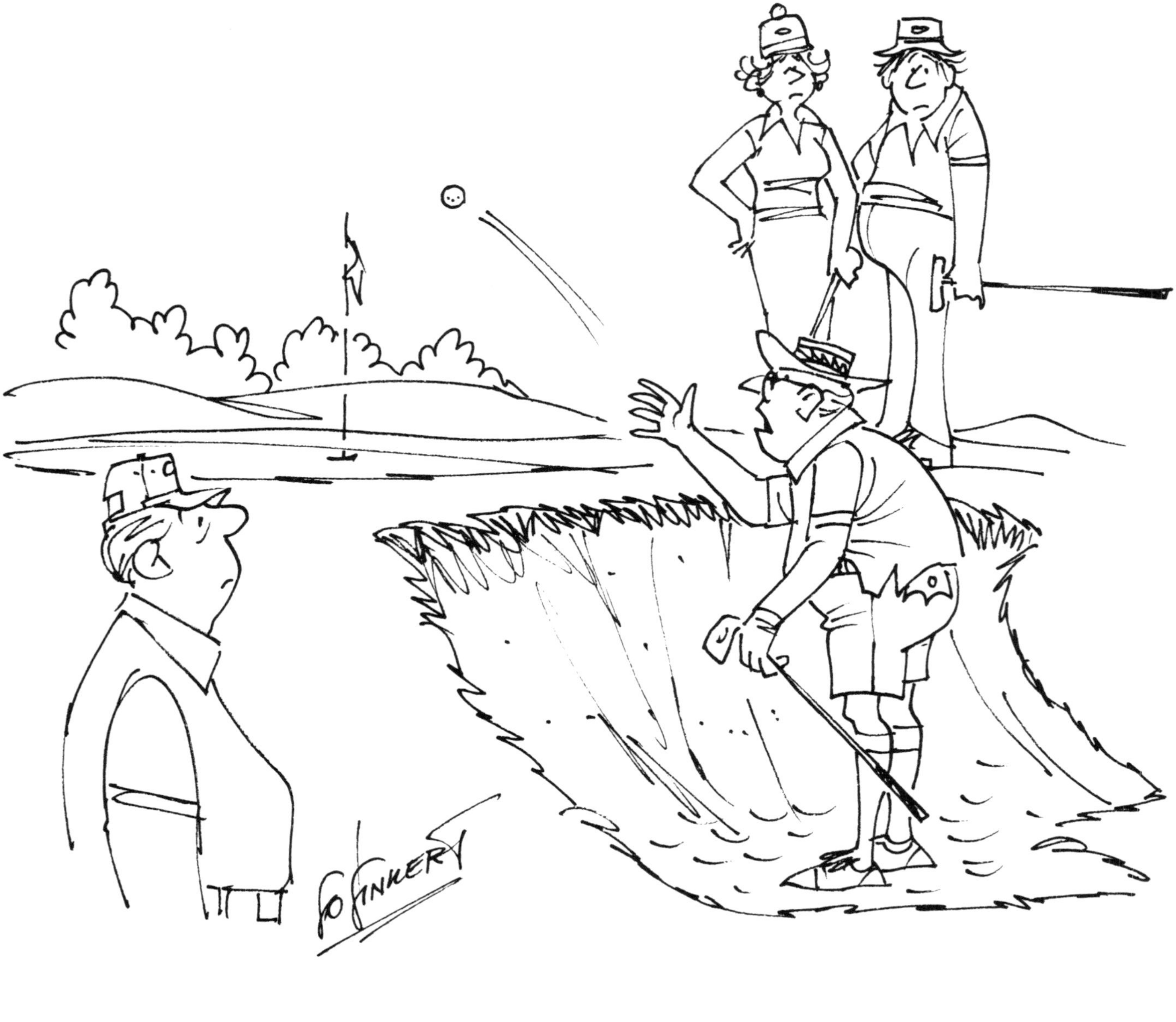

" AS A MATTER OF FACT I HAVE READ THE RULES, BUT THEY DON'T MAKE ANY SENSE TO ME!"

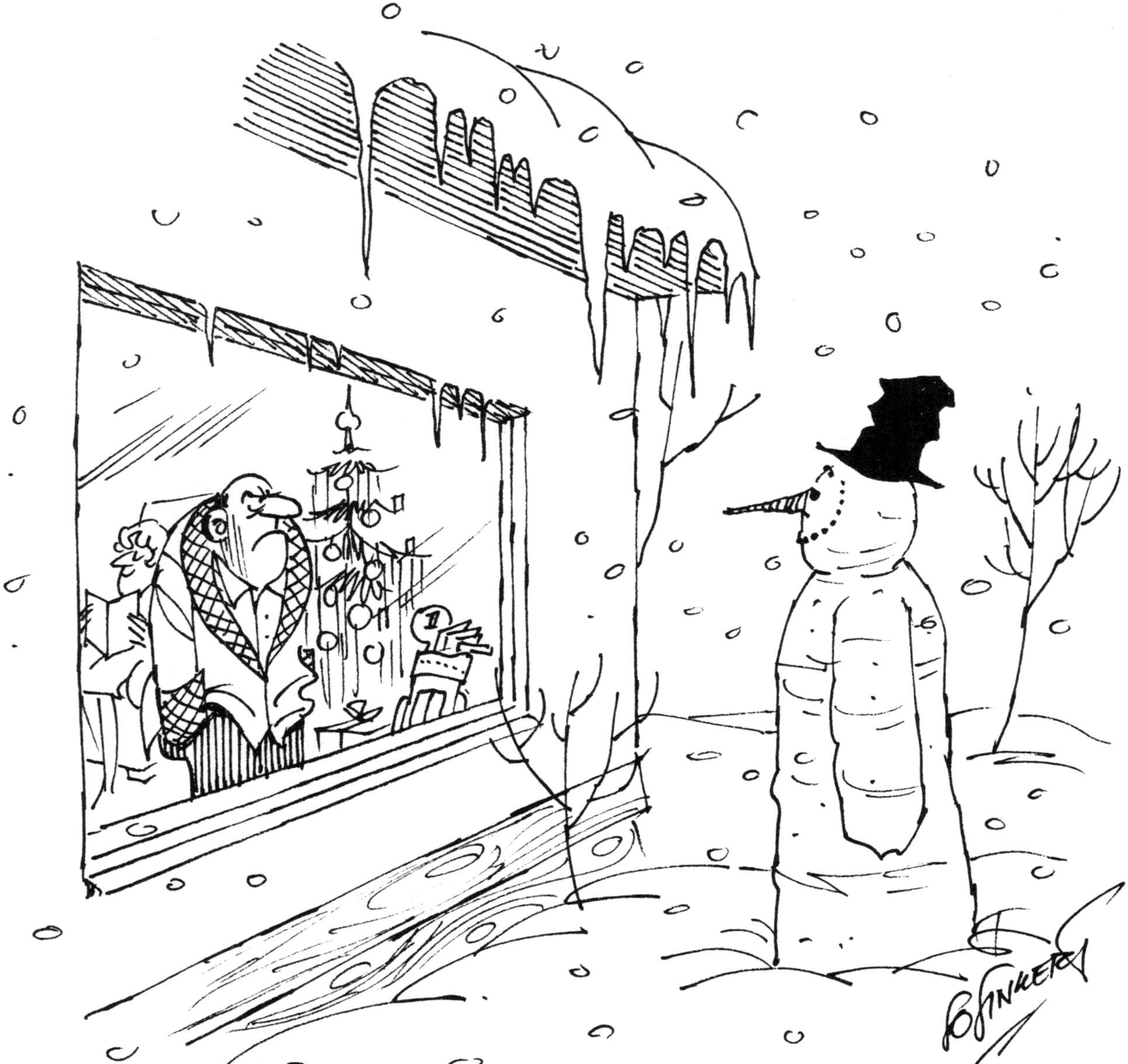

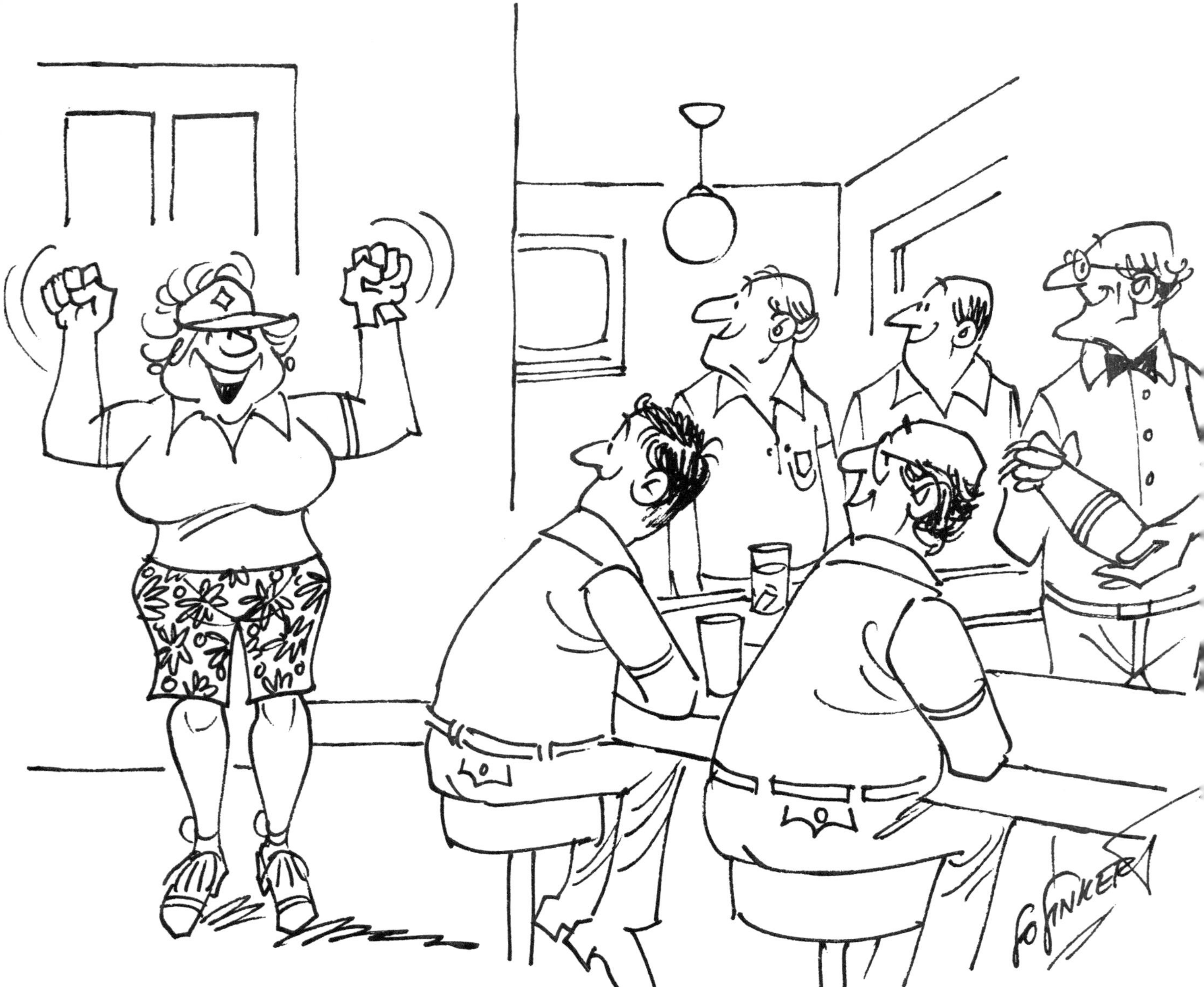

"TARRAH!.. THE DRINKS ARE ON ME, I CLOBBERED THE PRO!"

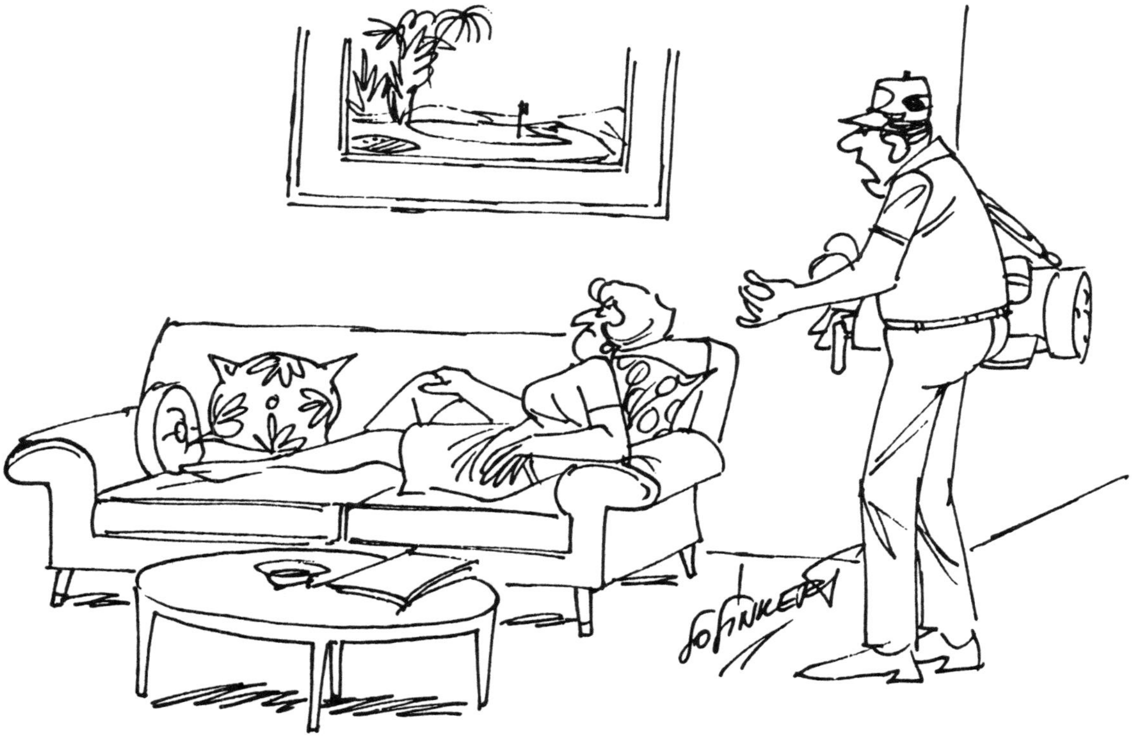
SOLFINKER

"SO I PLAYED 72 HOLES TODAY. THE TROUBLE WITH YOU, DEAR, IS THAT YOU TAKE MY GOLF TOO SERIOUSLY."

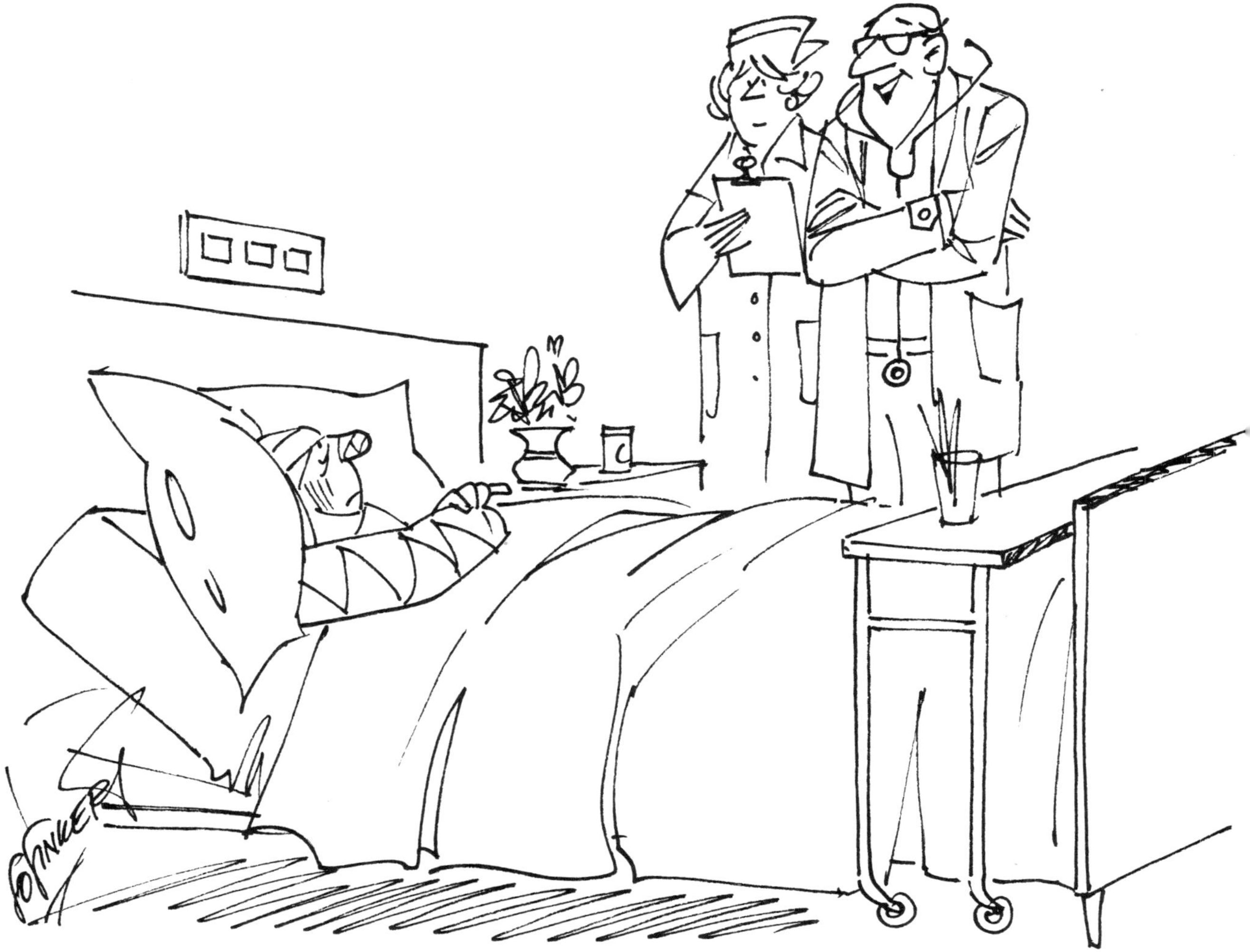
FOPINKER

"NEXT TIME YOU THROW YOUR GOLF CLUBS INTO A RAVINE LET GO OF THEM FIRST!"

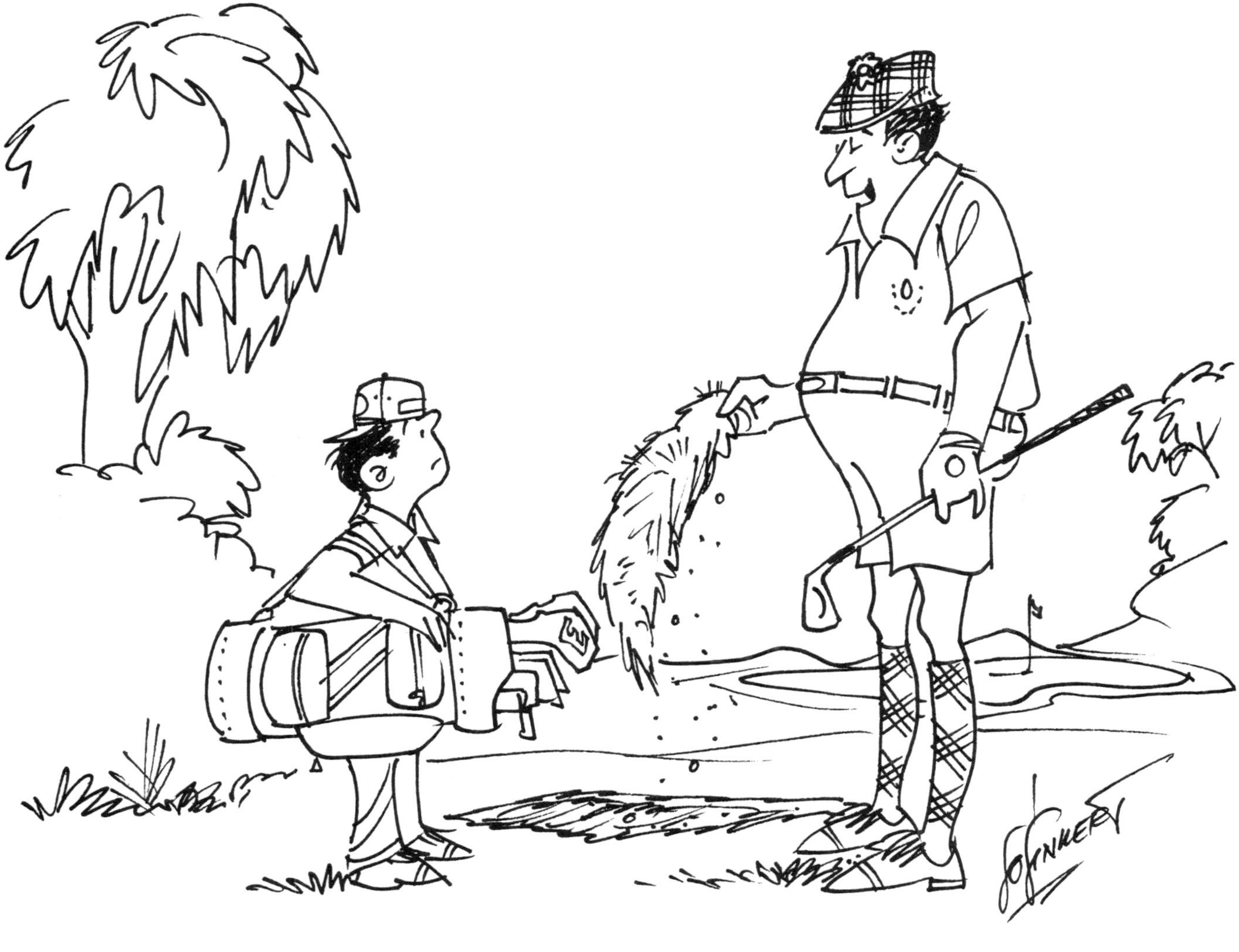

HERE, SLIP THIS IN MY GOLFBAG, I'M RE-SODDING GRANDPA'S GRAVE."

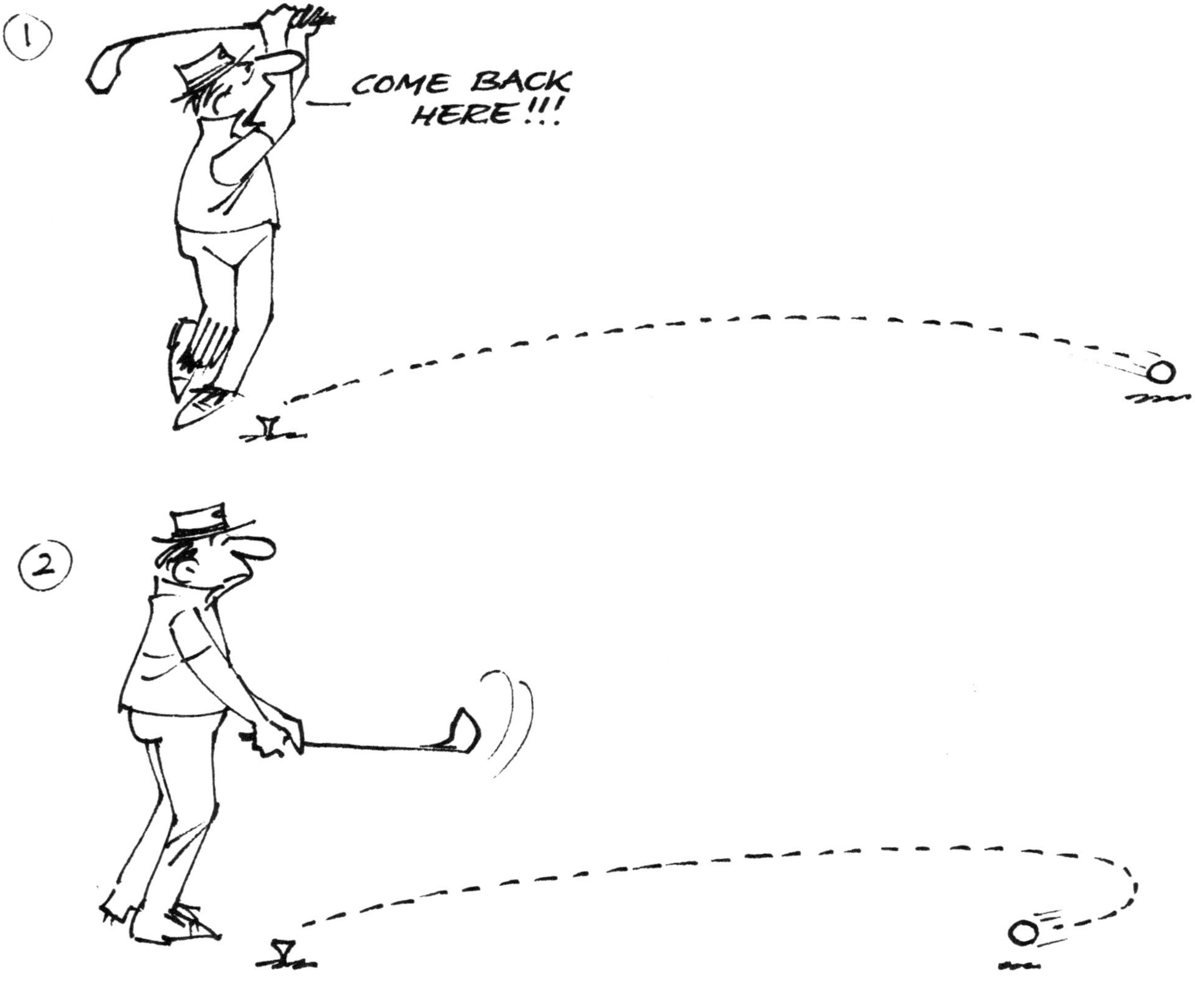
1
COME BACK HERE!!!
2

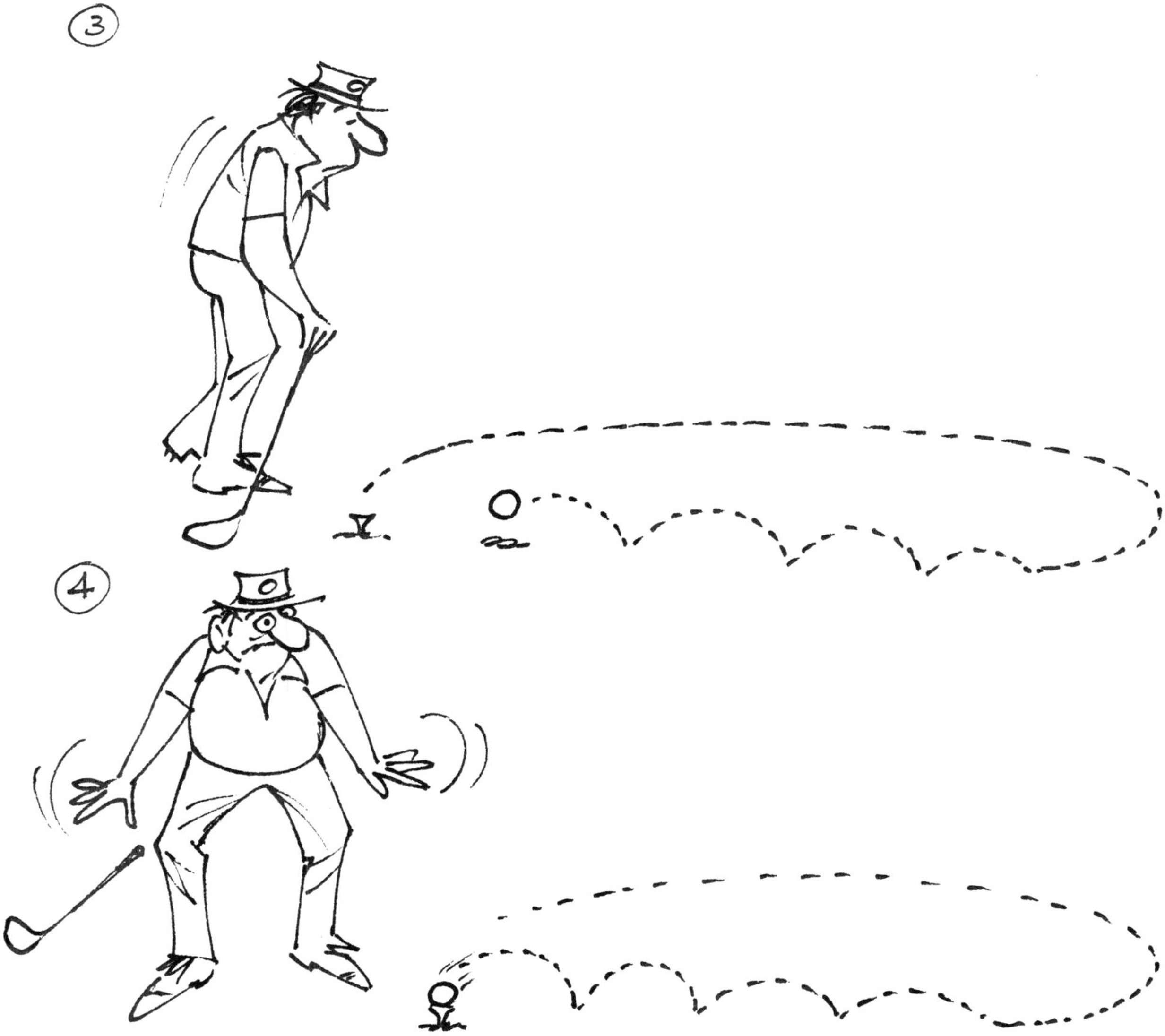
3
4

" HE MUST HAVE TAKEN THEM WITH HIM. "

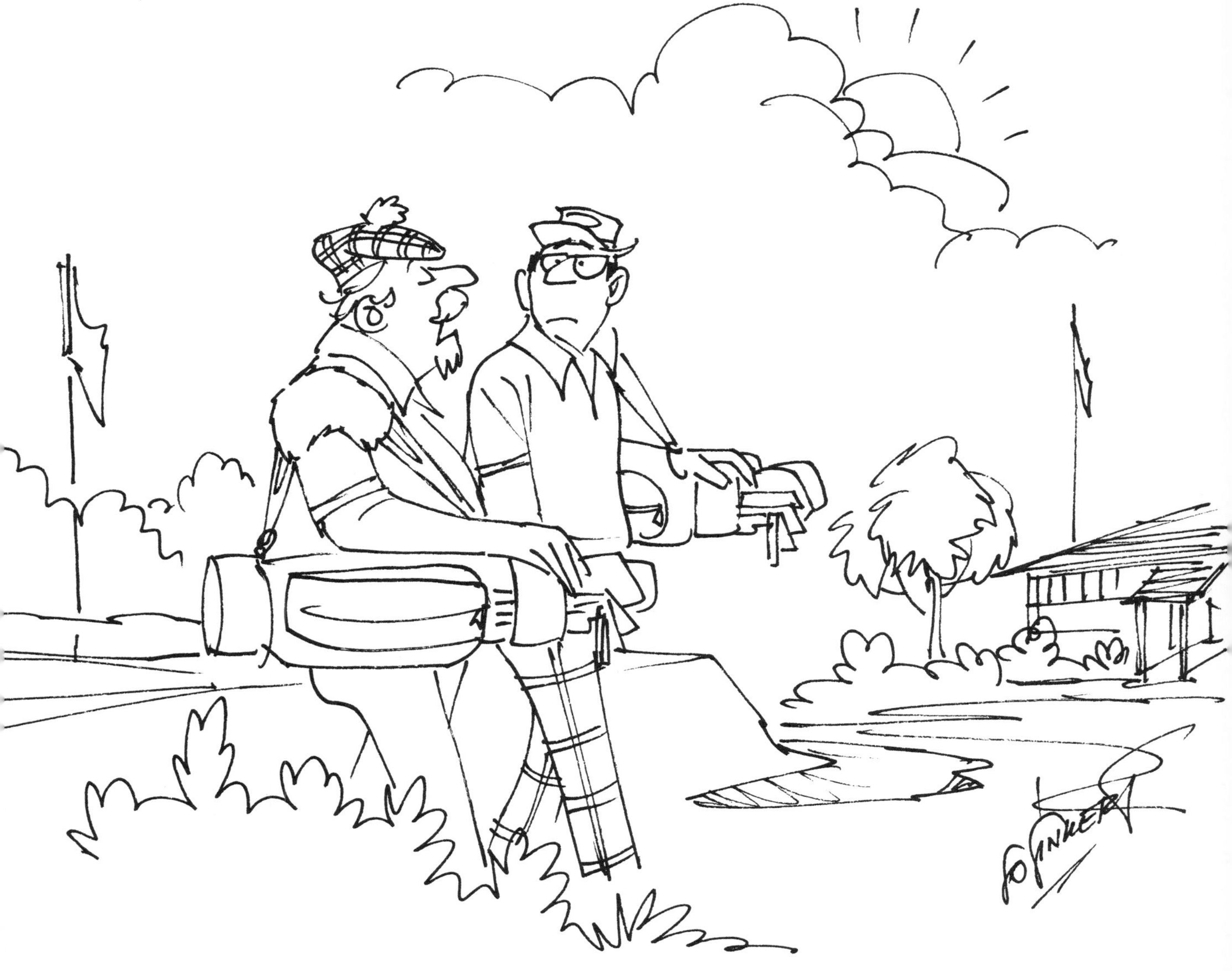

HARRIS YOU'RE A BETTER DRIVER THAN ME, A BETTER CHIPPER AND A BETTER PUTTER AND YOU BETTER FIND YOURSELF A BETTER JOB!"

1

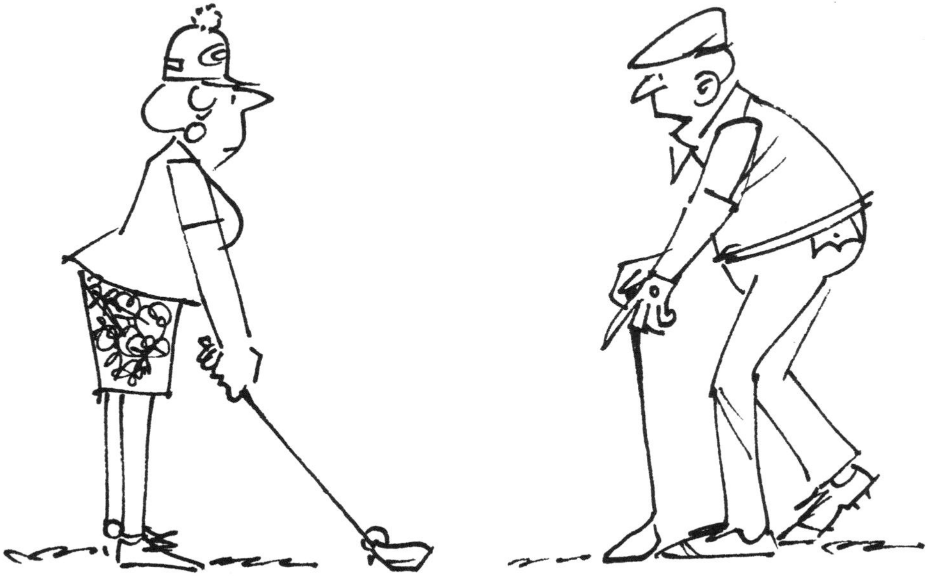

2

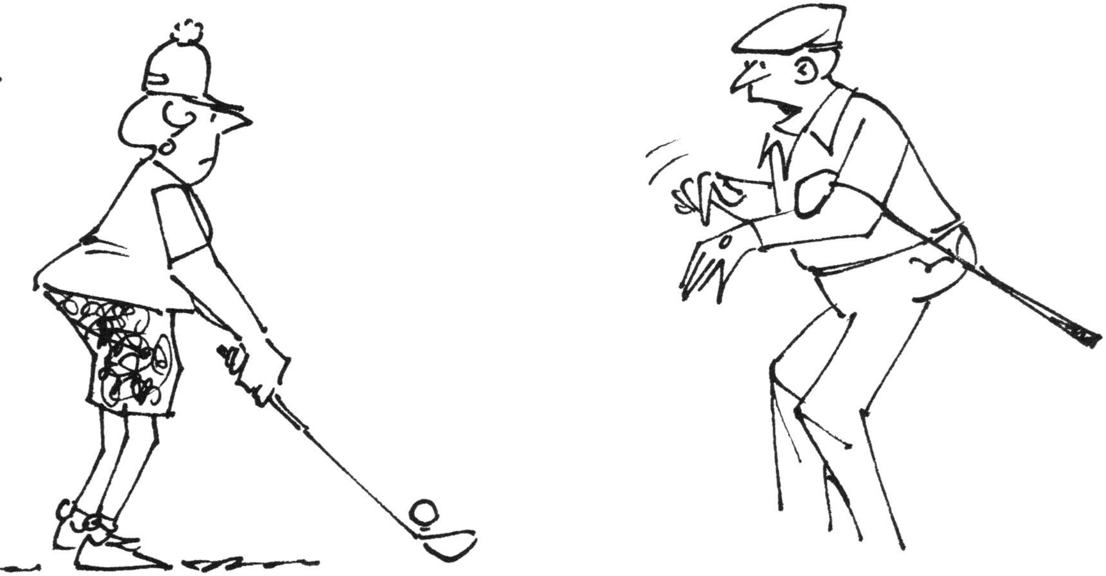

3

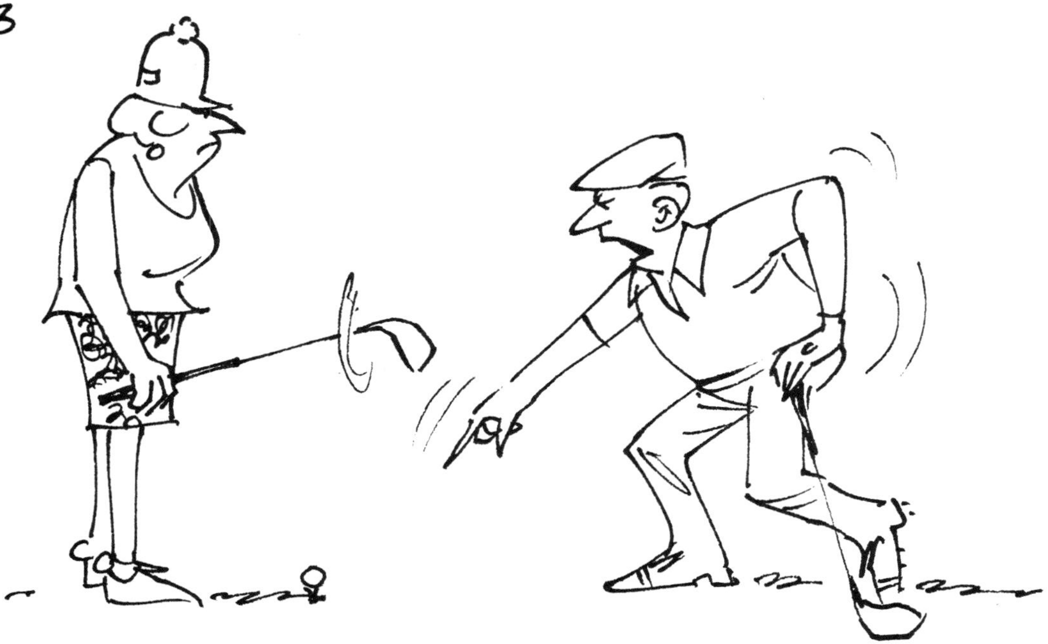

4

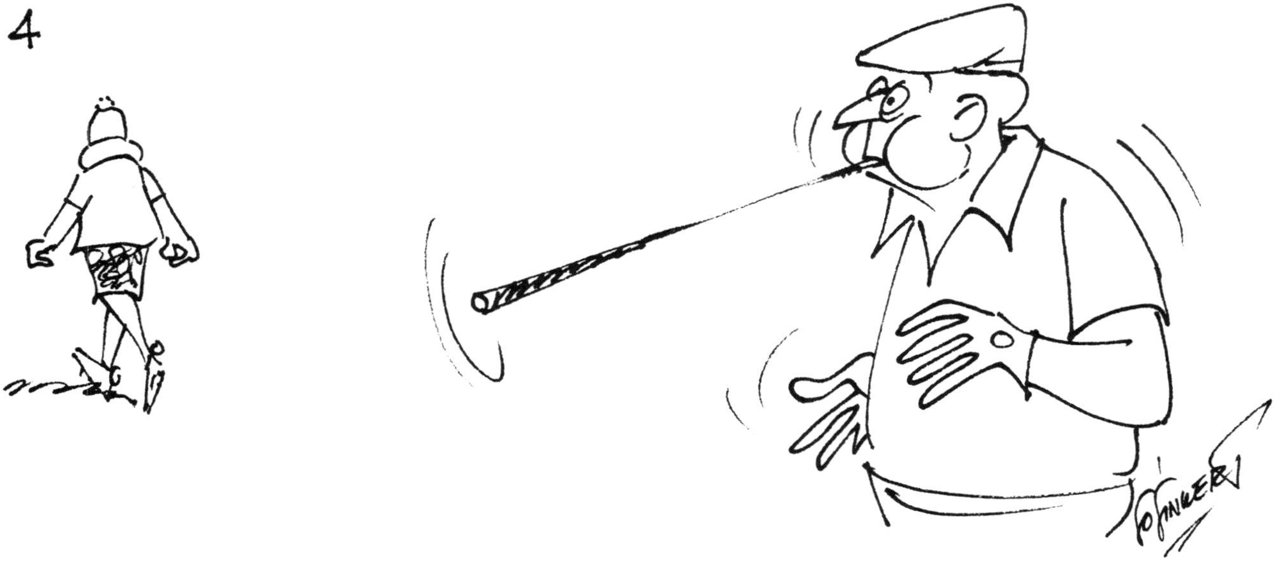

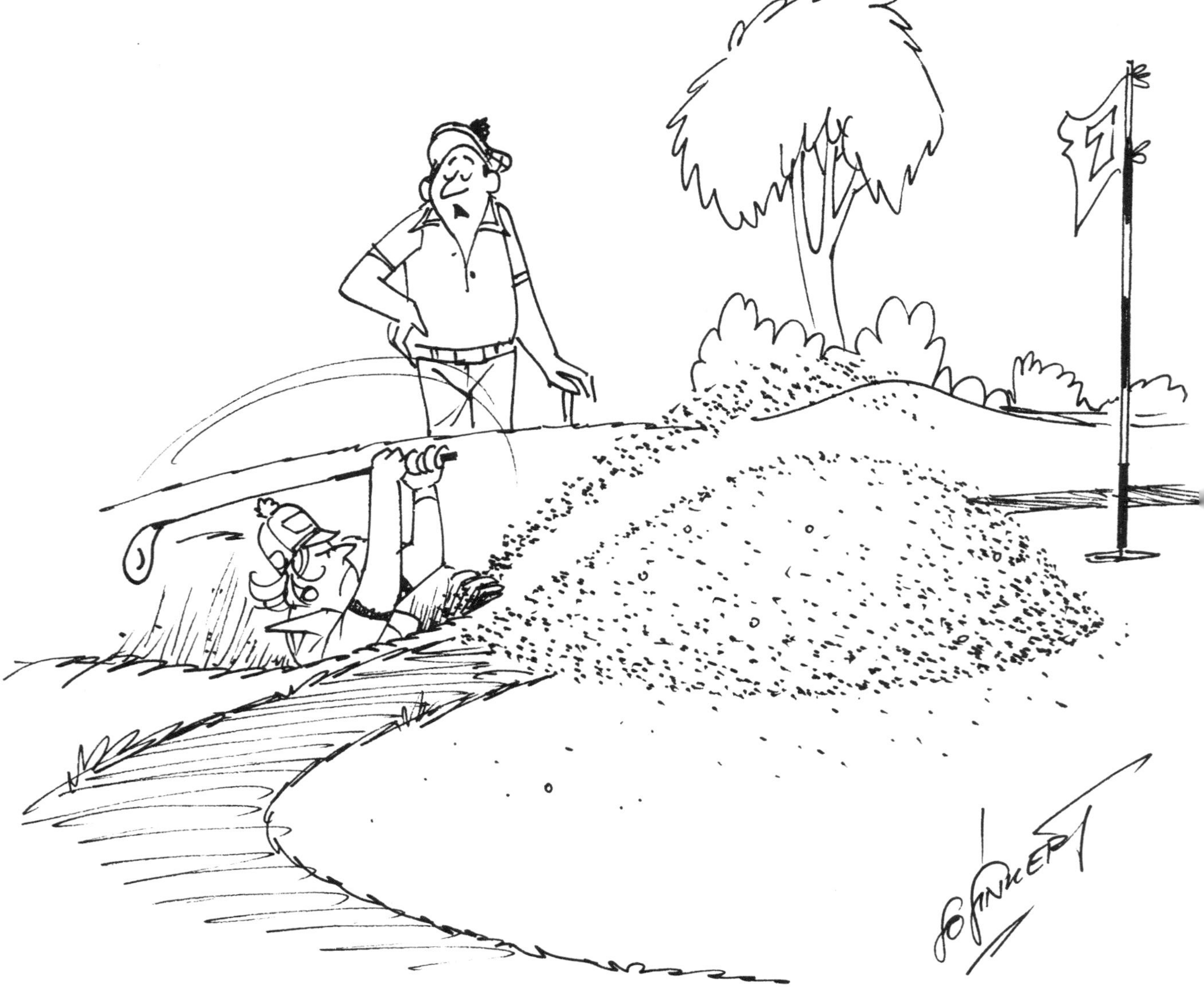

"YOU'D BETTER PICK UP YOUR BALL, BERTHA. WE HAVE TO LEAVE A LITTLE SAND IN THE BUNKER FOR THE OTHER GOLFERS."

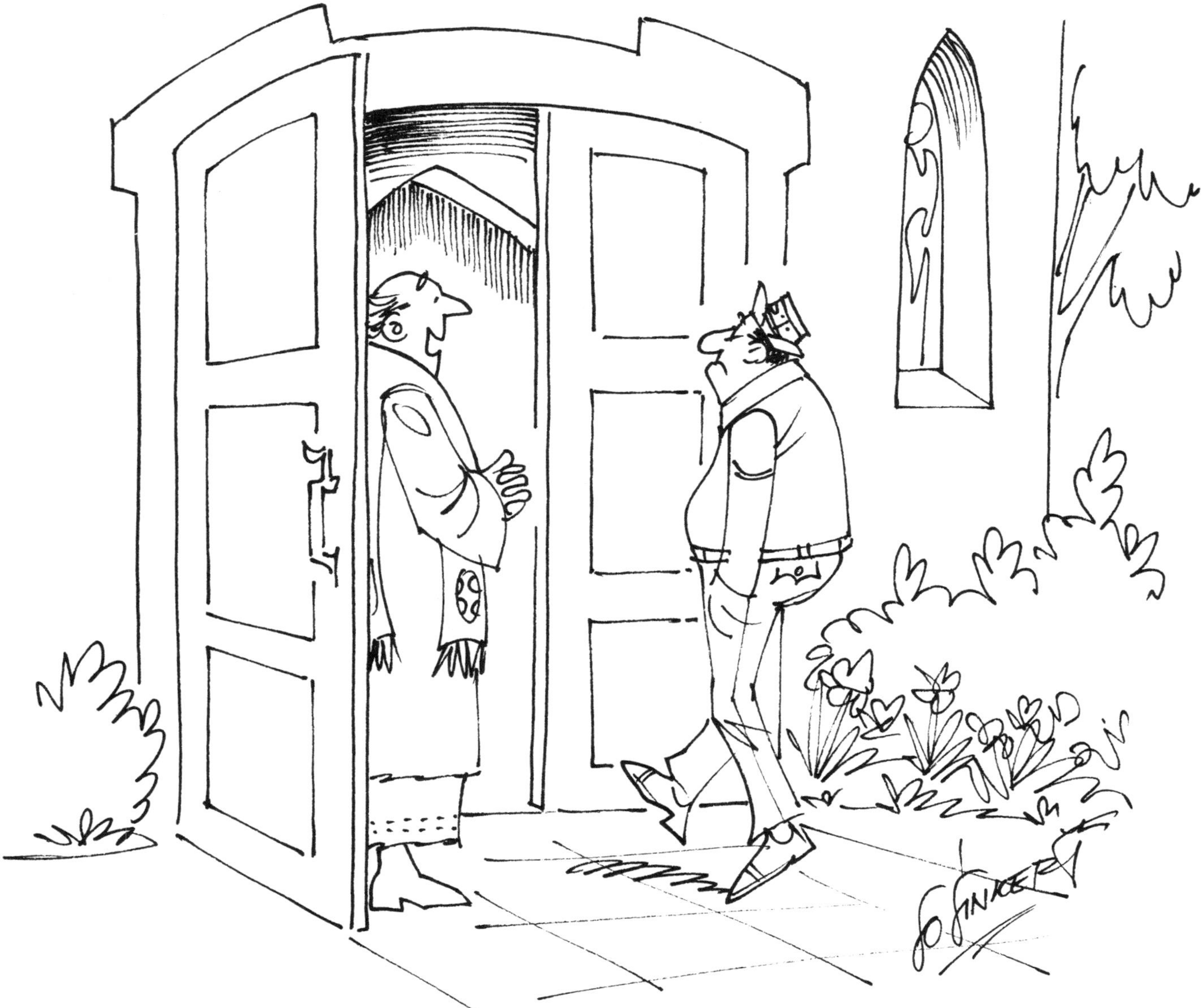

"WELL, MR DOUGLAS, SECOND THOUGHTS OR OVERCROWDED GOLF COURSE?"

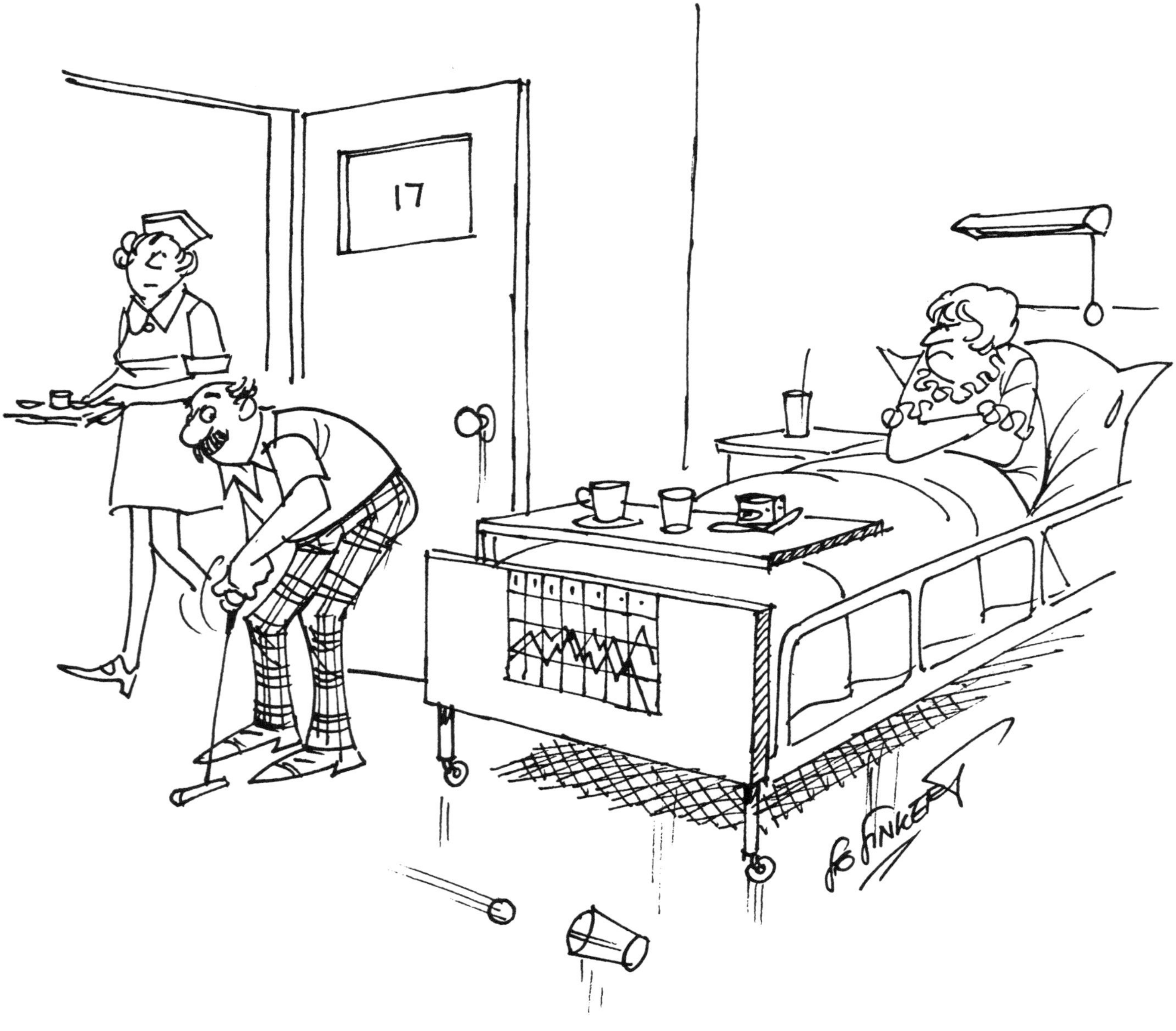
17
Jo Tinker

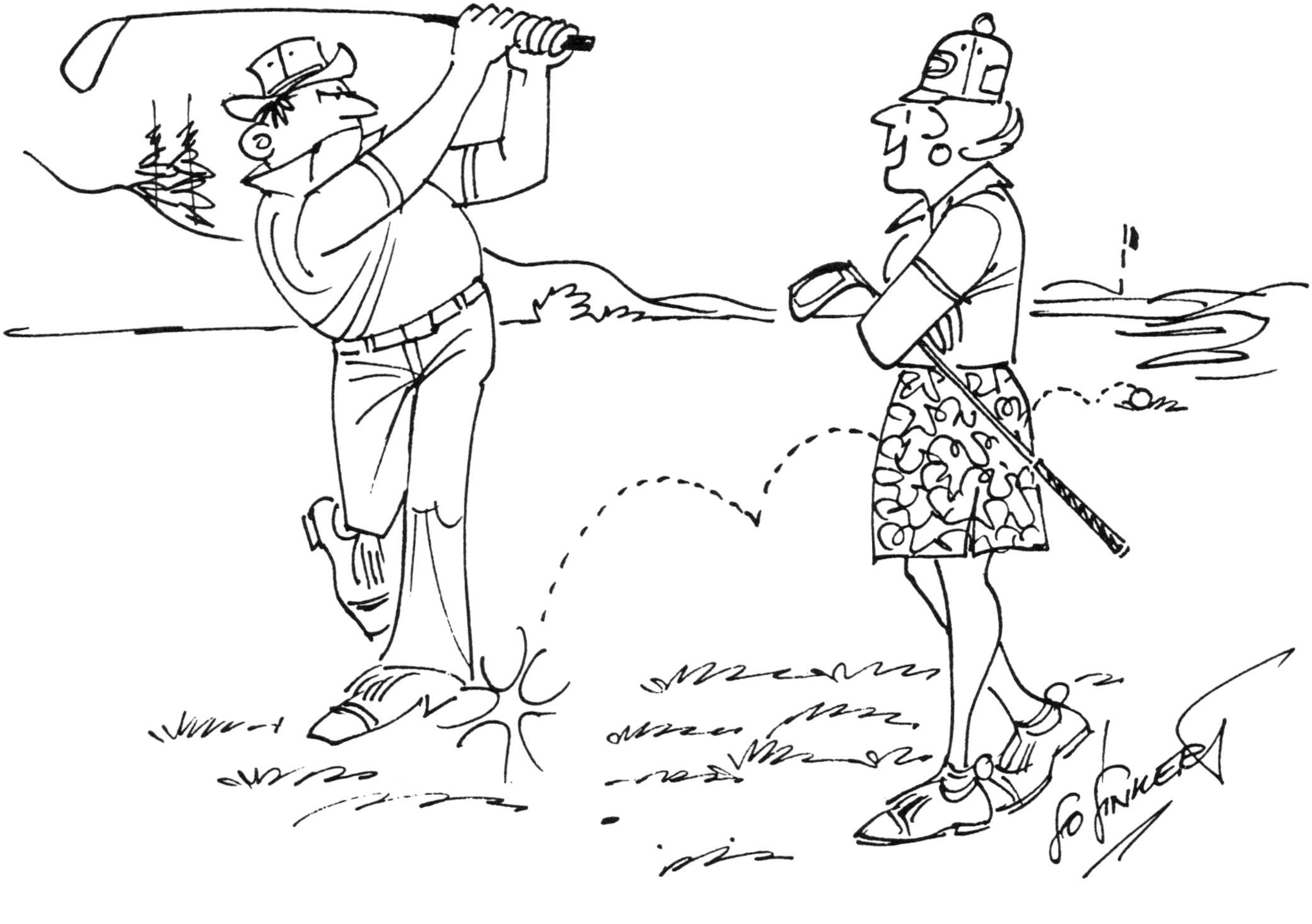

"THAT'S A GREAT DRIVE . . . . FOR MINIATURE GOLF!'"

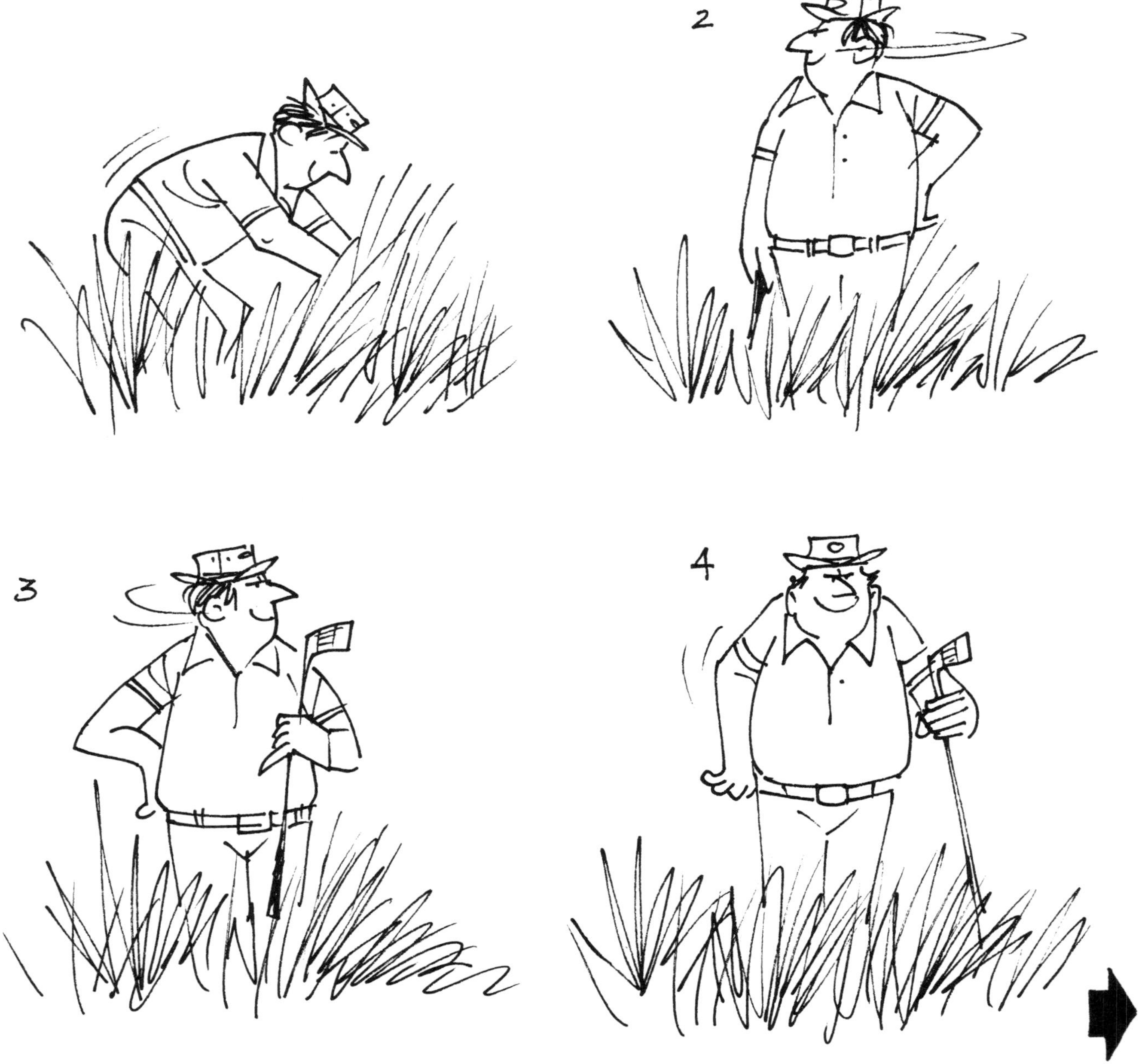
2
3
4

5

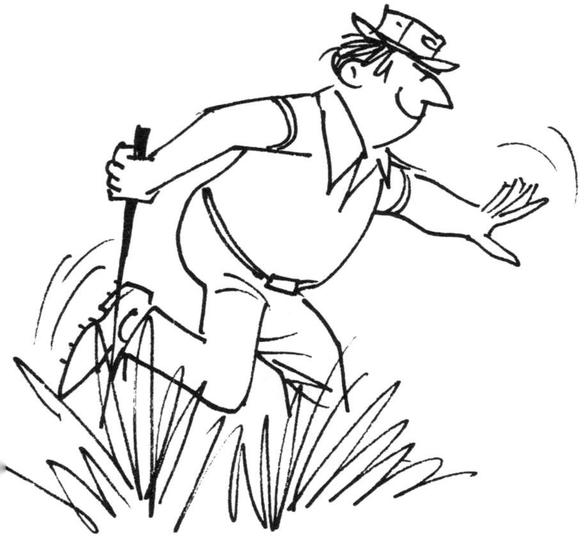

6

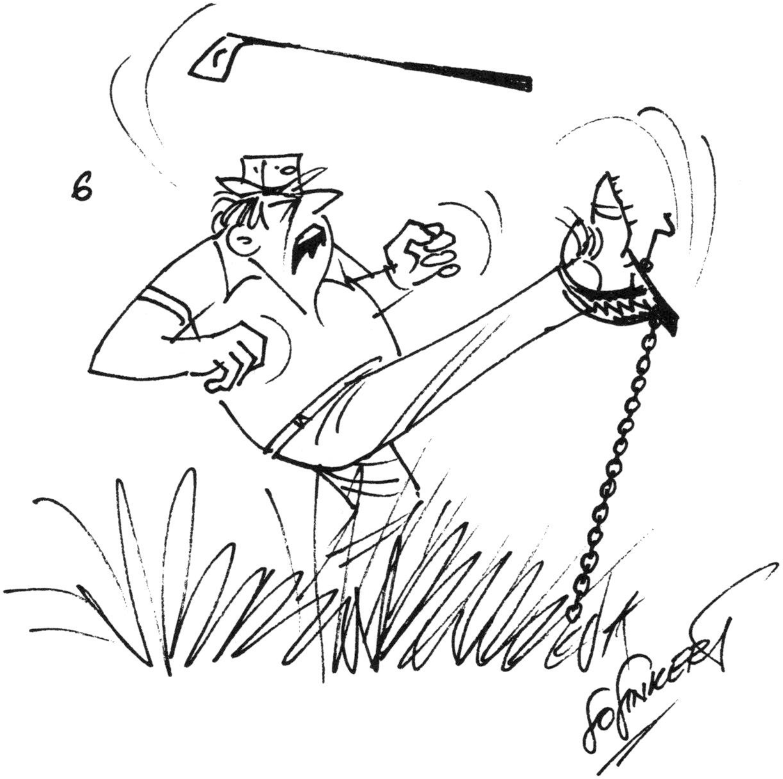

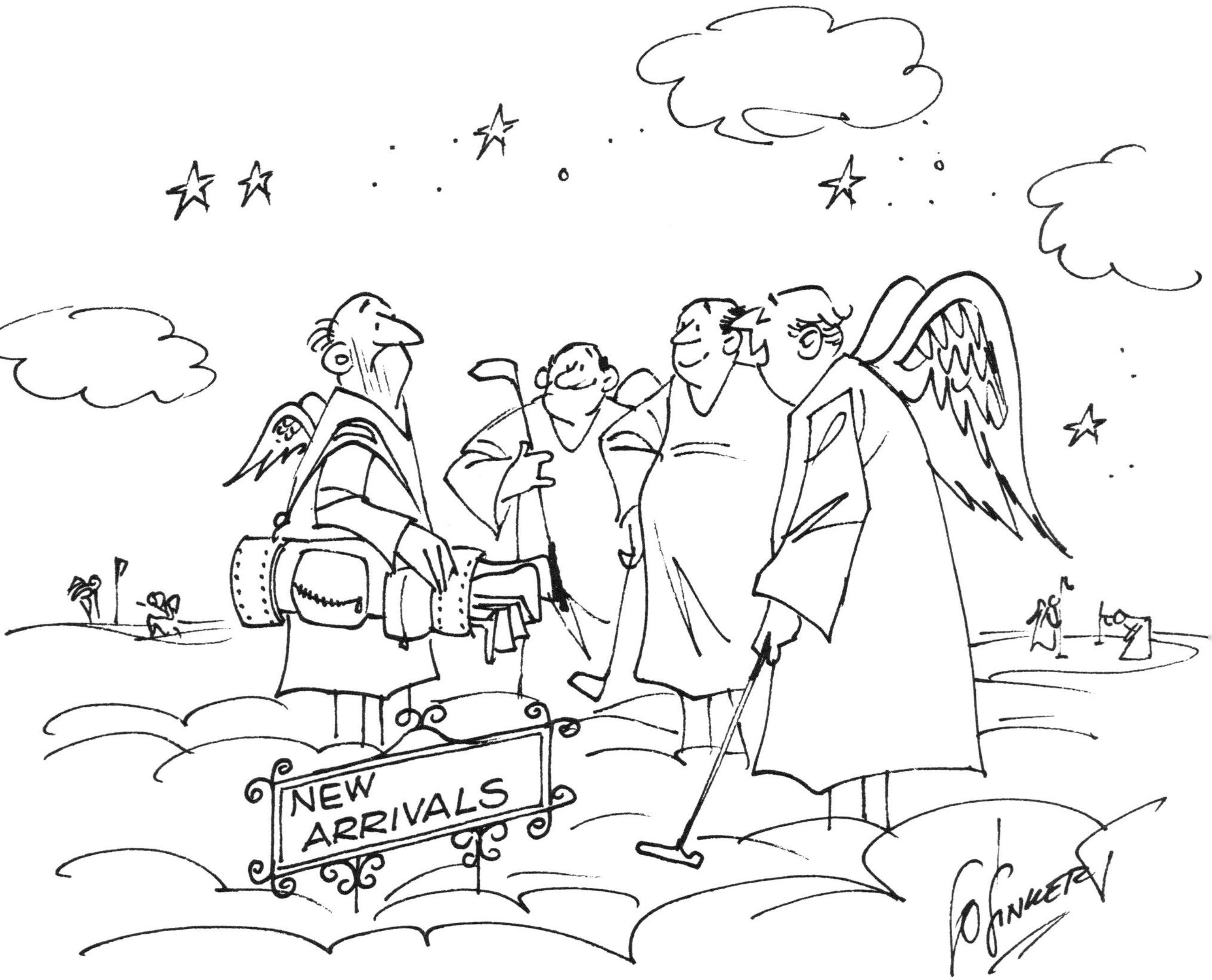
NEW
ARRIVALS

" WELCOME TO THE HEAVENLY PASTURES. SORRY TO TELL YOU WE'RE ON A FIVE-YEAR WAITING LIST."

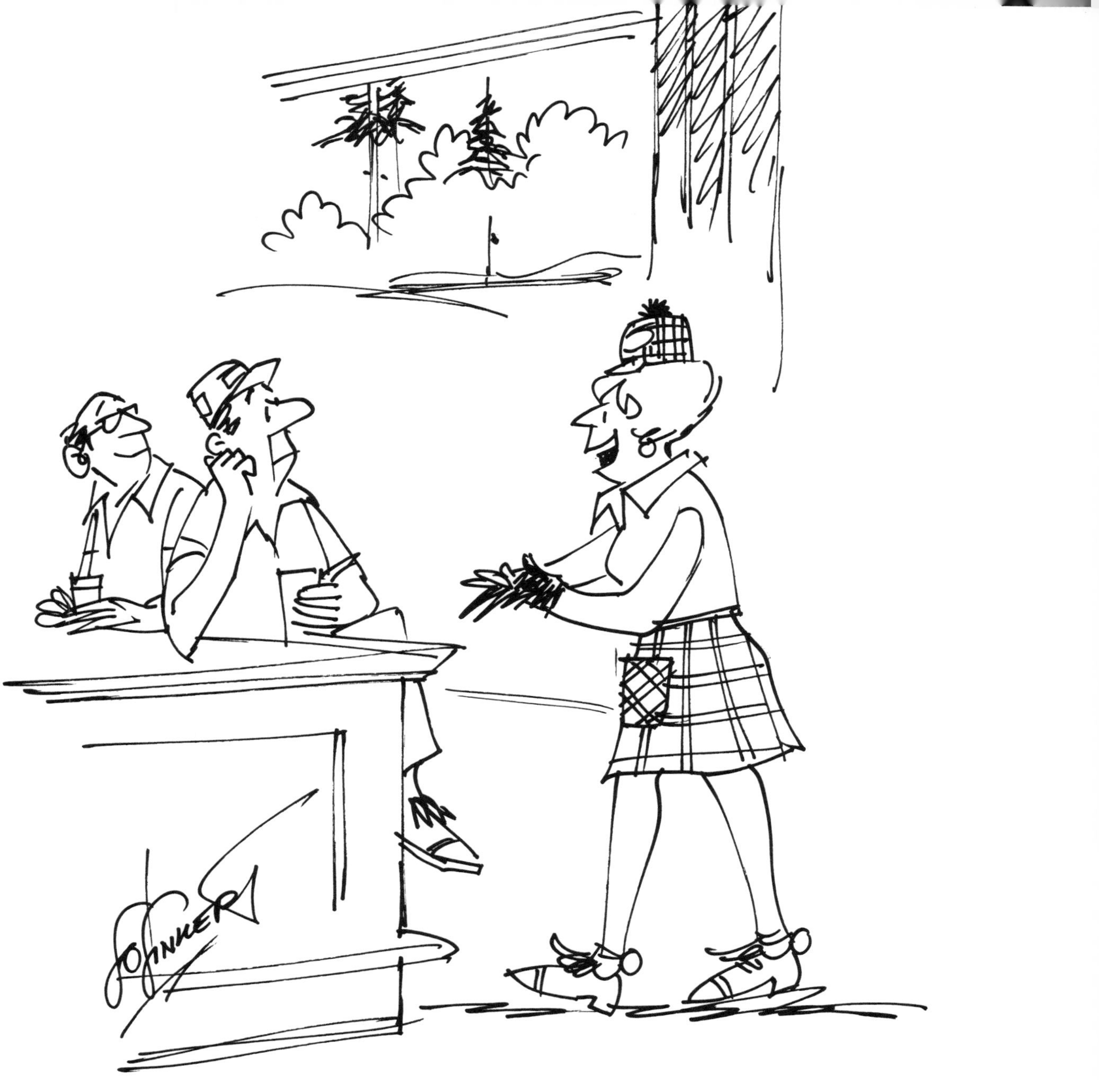
JO PINKER

" BUY ME A DRINK, DARLING, I CAME IN SECOND IN OUR TWOSOME."

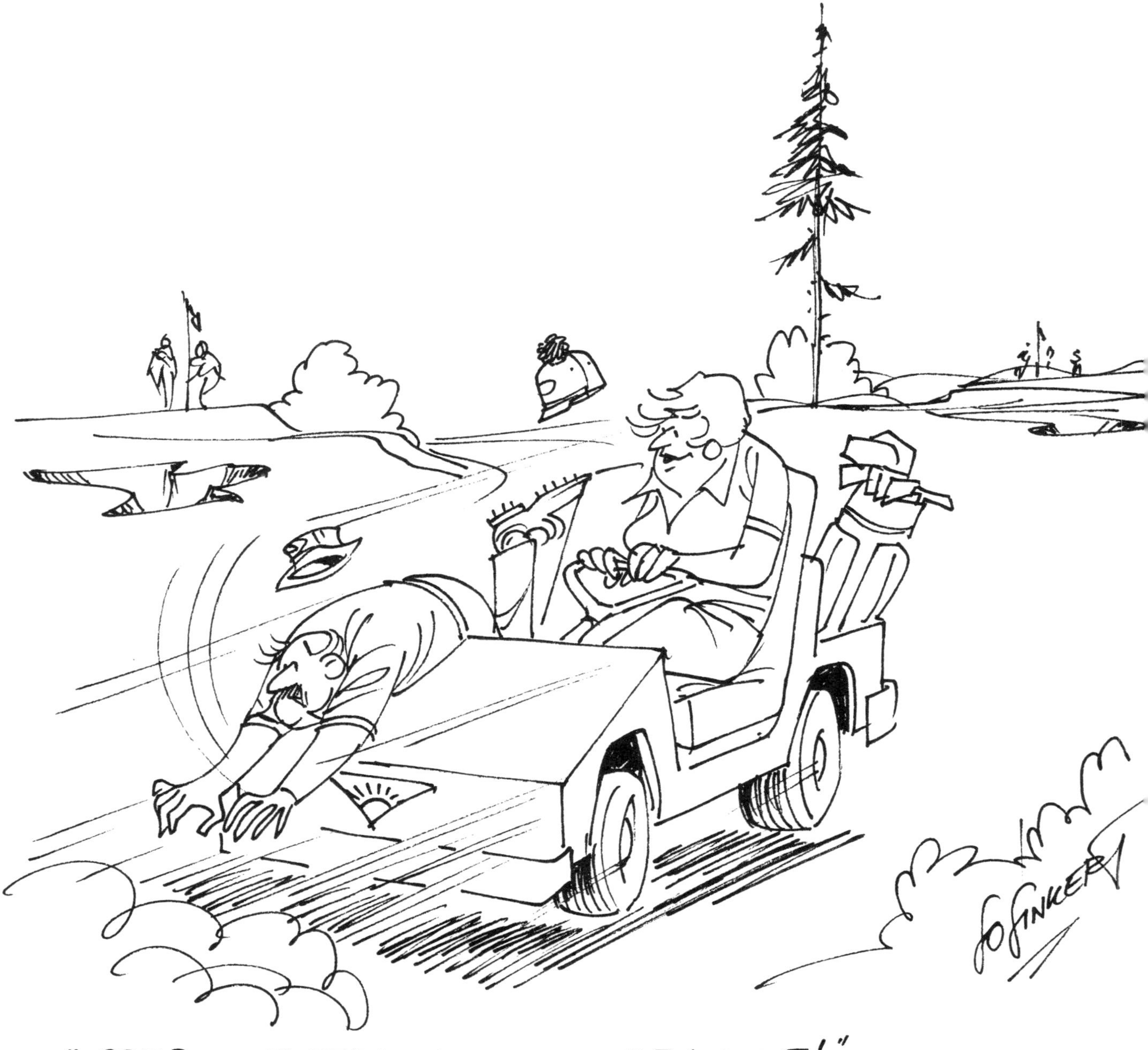

" OOPS . . . I STILL HAD IT IN REVERSE! "

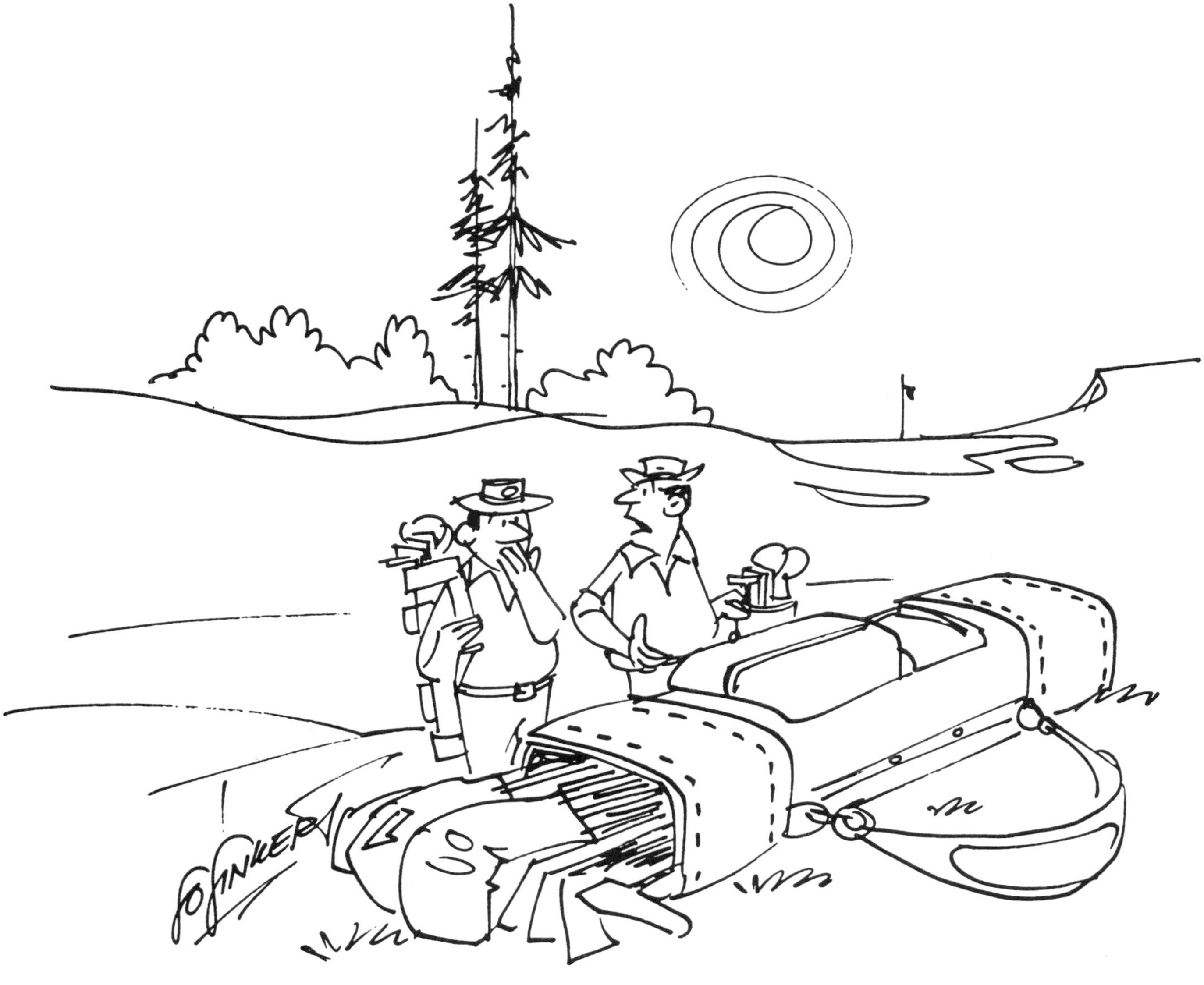

NO, I DON'T KNOW WHO OWNS THEM BUT I THINK WE BETTER LET HIM PLAY THROUGH!"

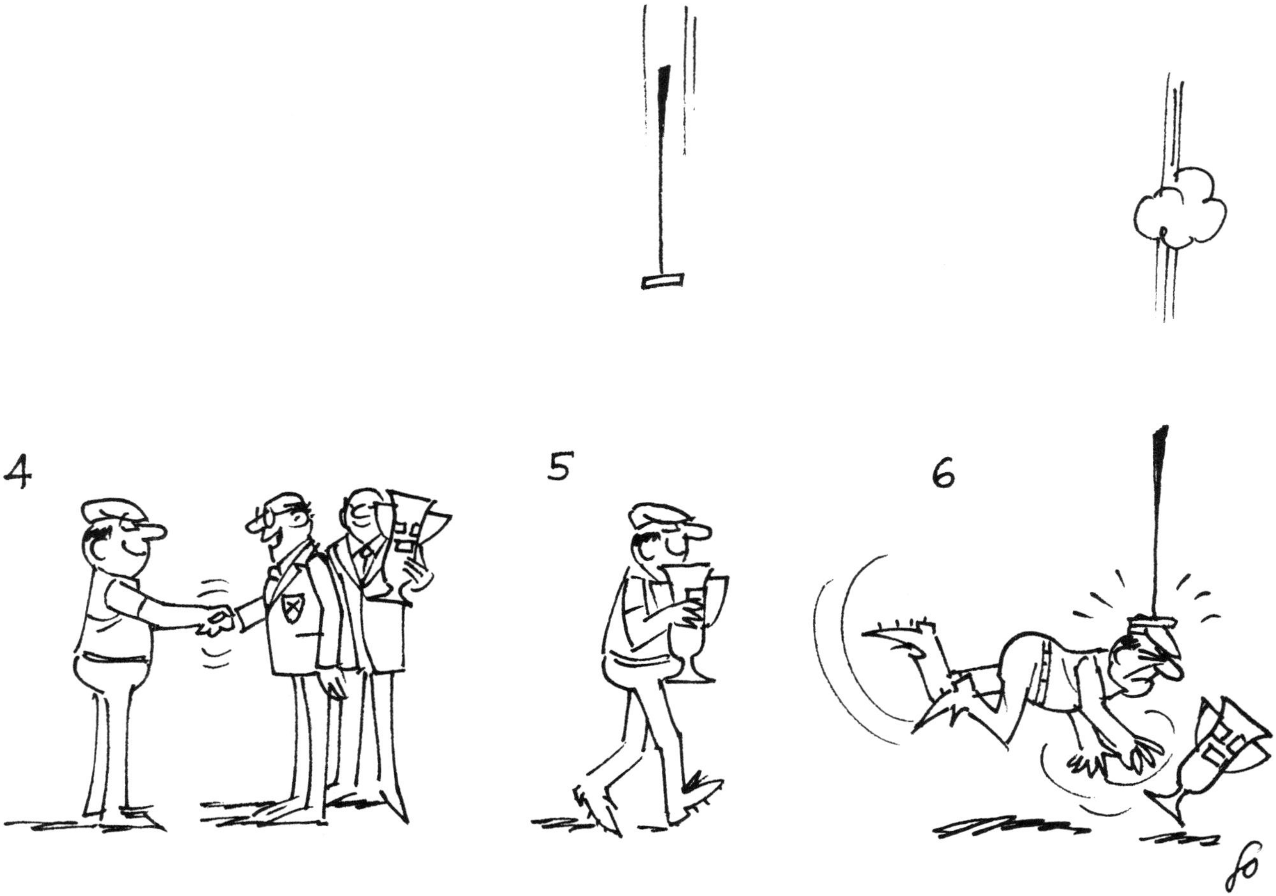
4
5
6

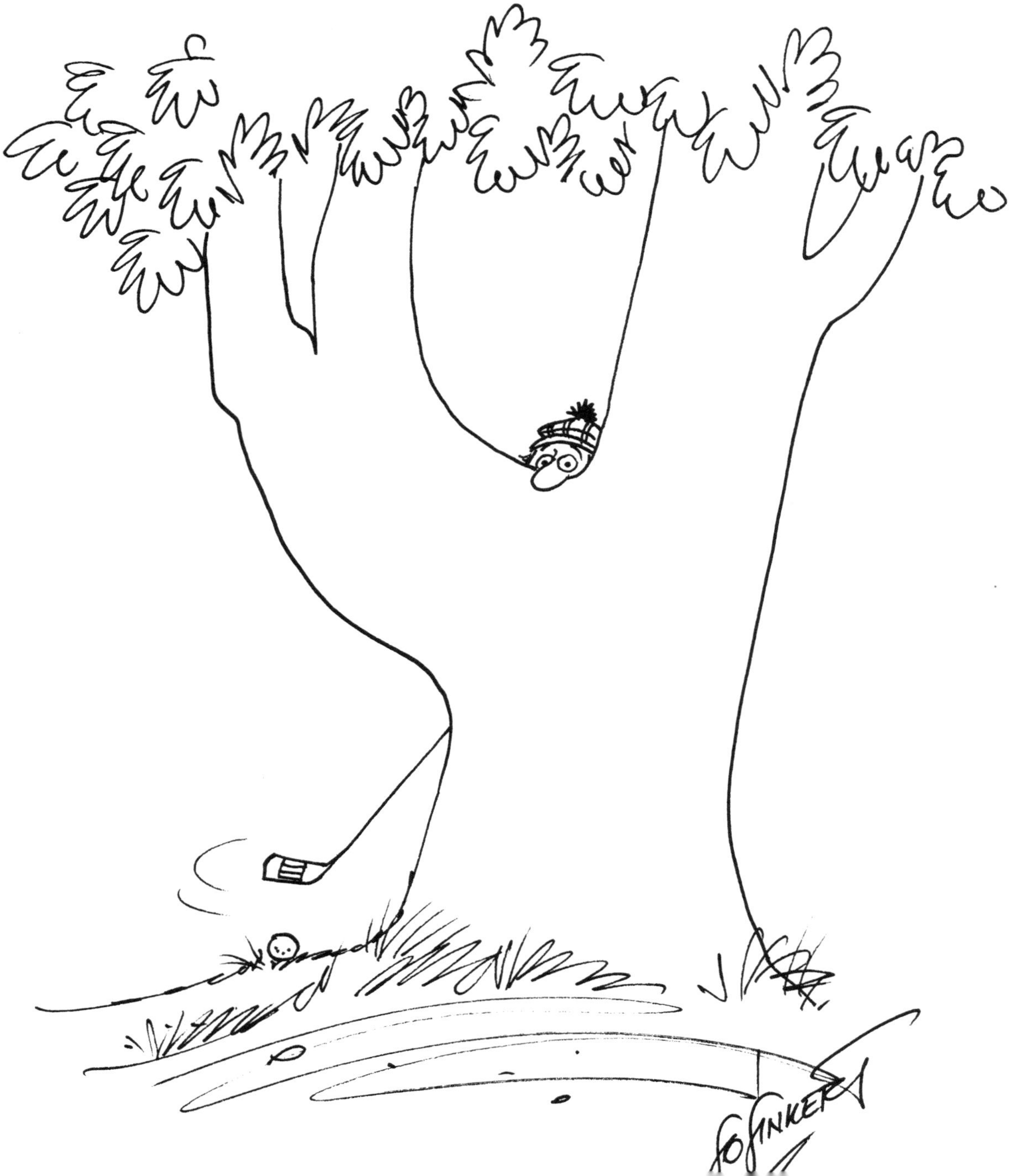

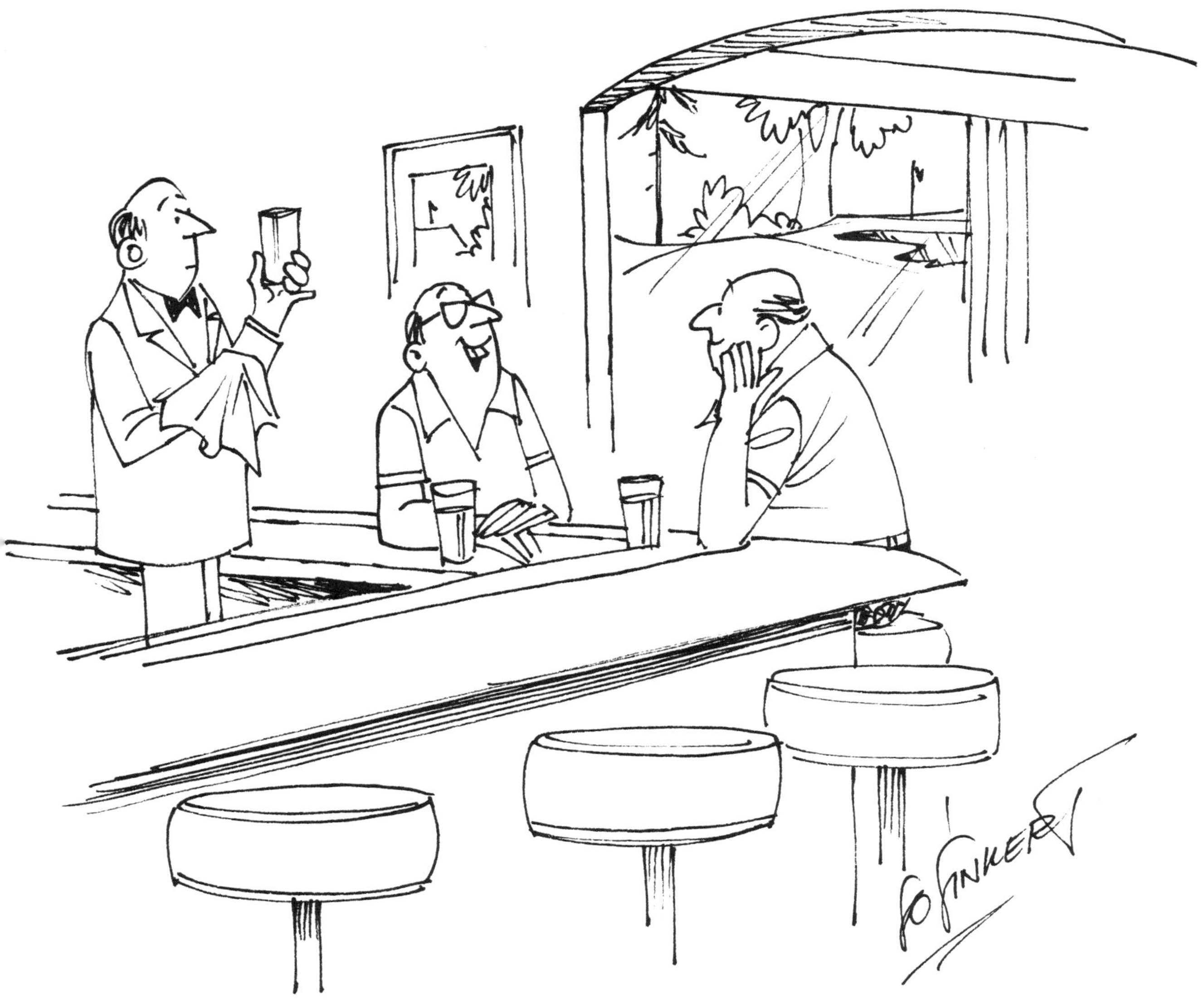
FO SINKER

" I TOOK LESSONS FROM THE PRO TODAY... HE SAID HE DIDN'T HAVE THE HEART TO CHARGE ME."

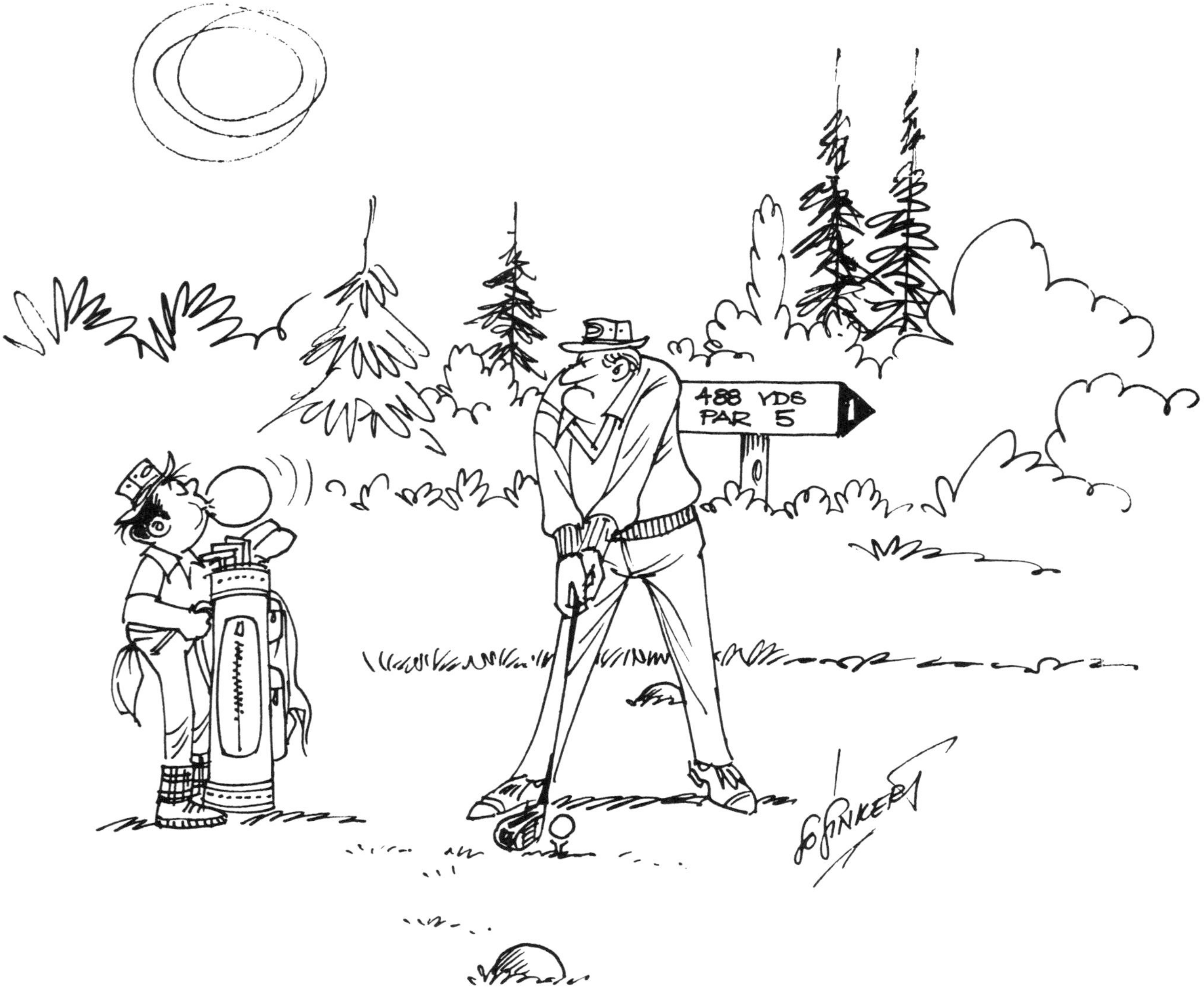
488 YDS
PAR 5
1

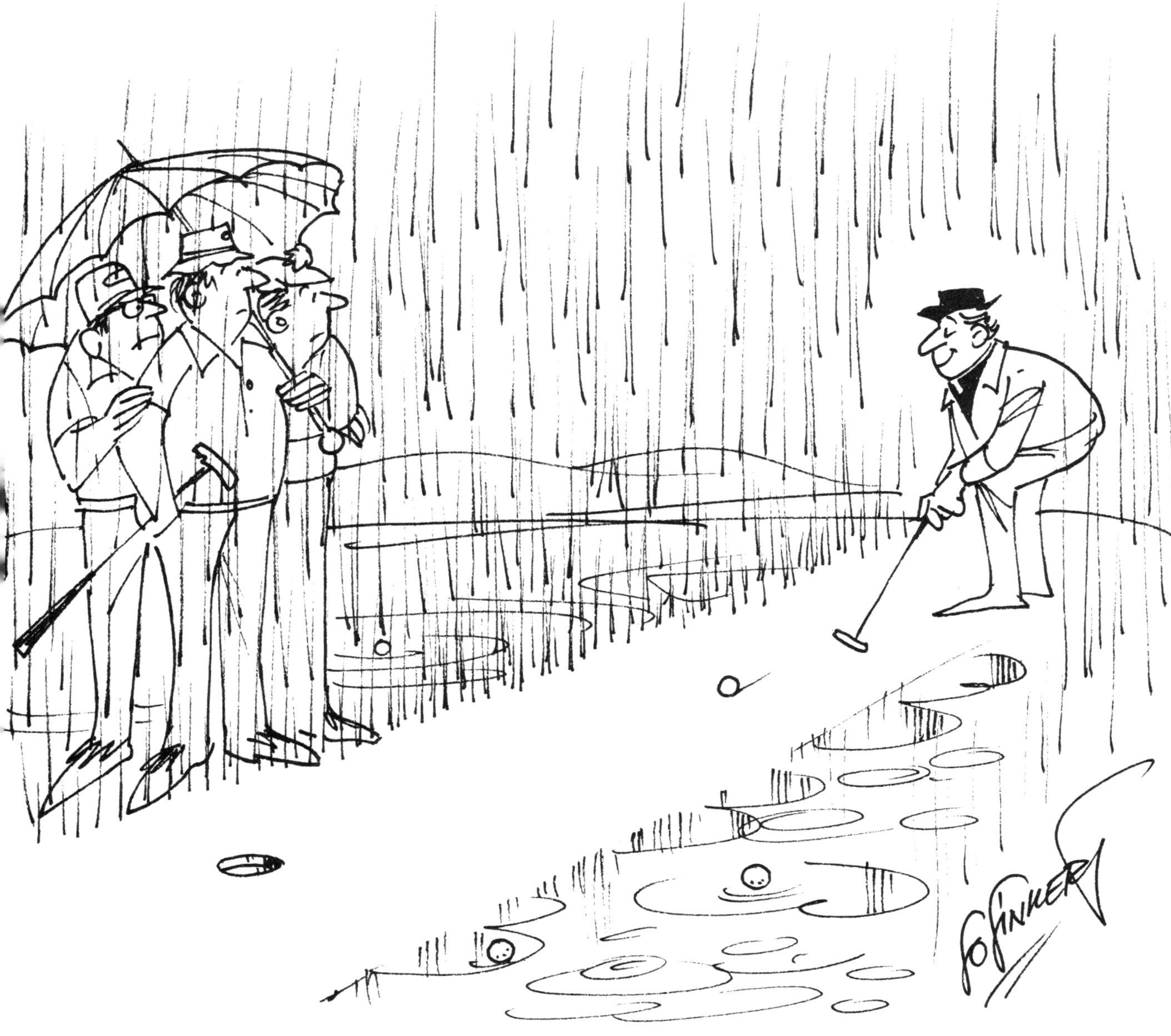

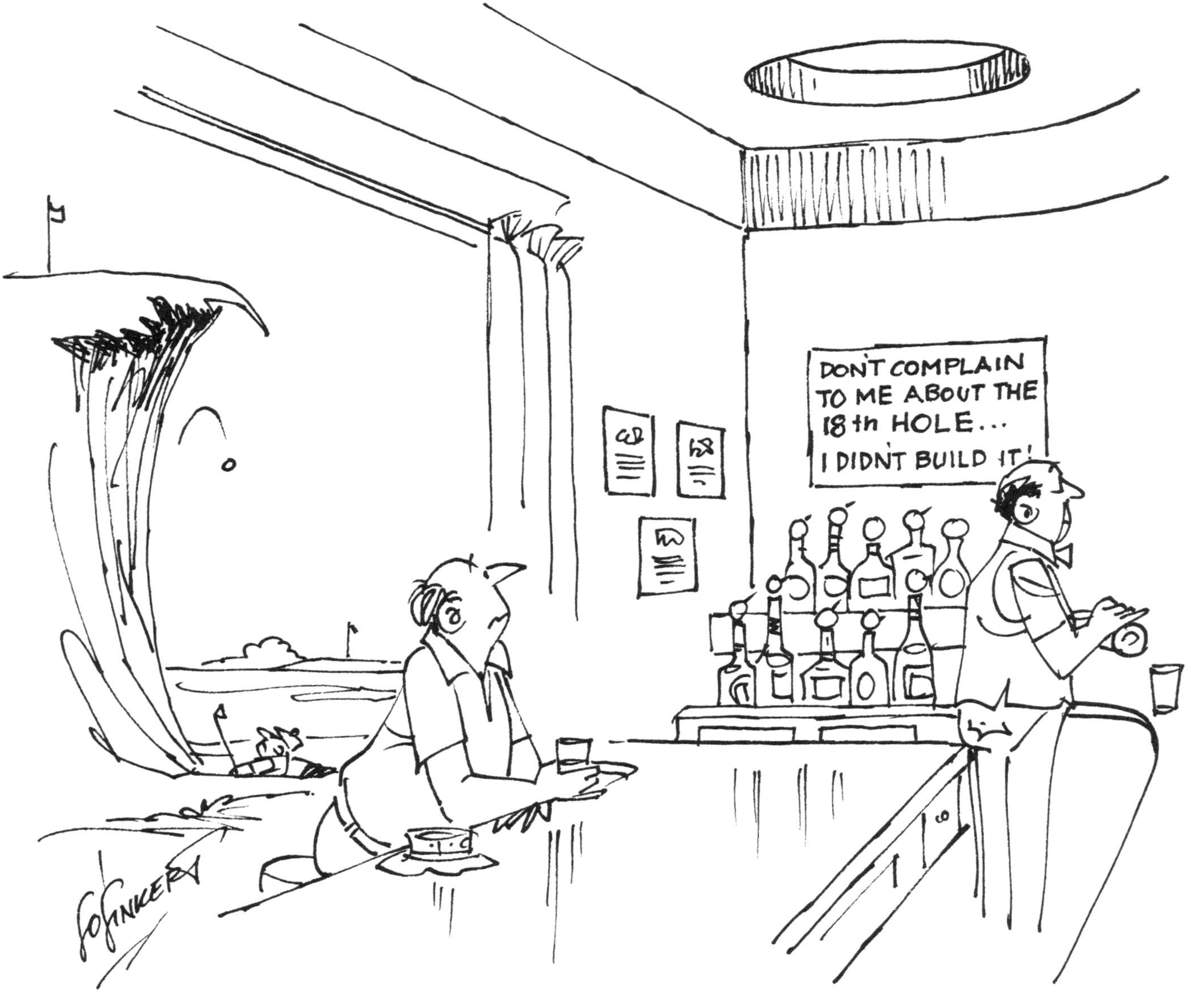
DON'T COMPLAIN TO ME ABOUT THE 18th HOLE...
I DIDN'T BUILD IT!

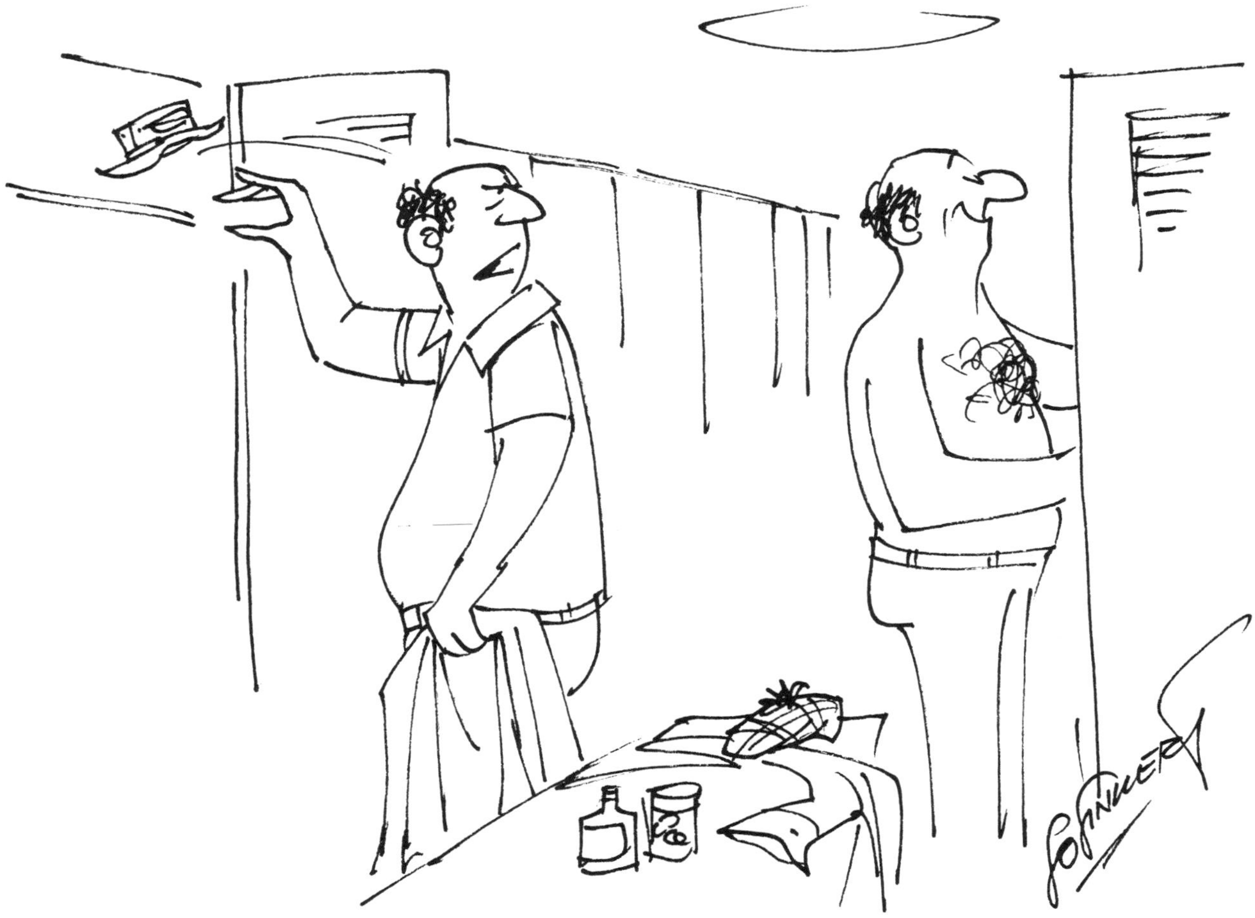

" THAT'S WHY I NEVER LIKE TO PLAY IN THE MORNING, IT SPOILS THE WHOLE DAY!"

"ASIDE FROM THOSE FOURTEEN HOLES WHERE YOU HAPPENED TO SCORE BETTER THAN I DID, WE WERE VERY EVENLY MATCHED."

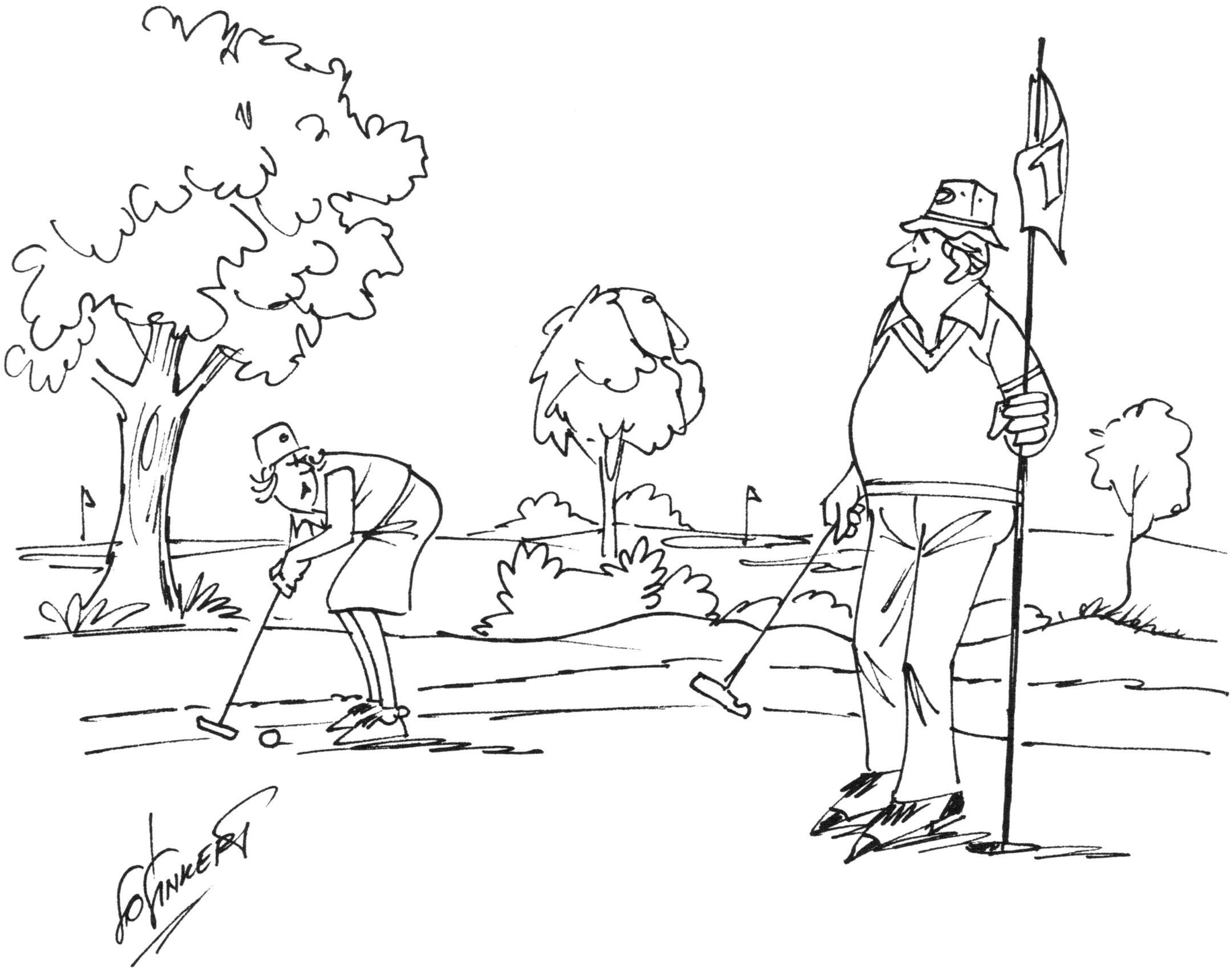

"STANDING IN MY LINE DOESN'T BOTHER ME, IT'S YOUR NEGATIVE FACIAL EXPRESSION THAT THROWS ME OFF!"

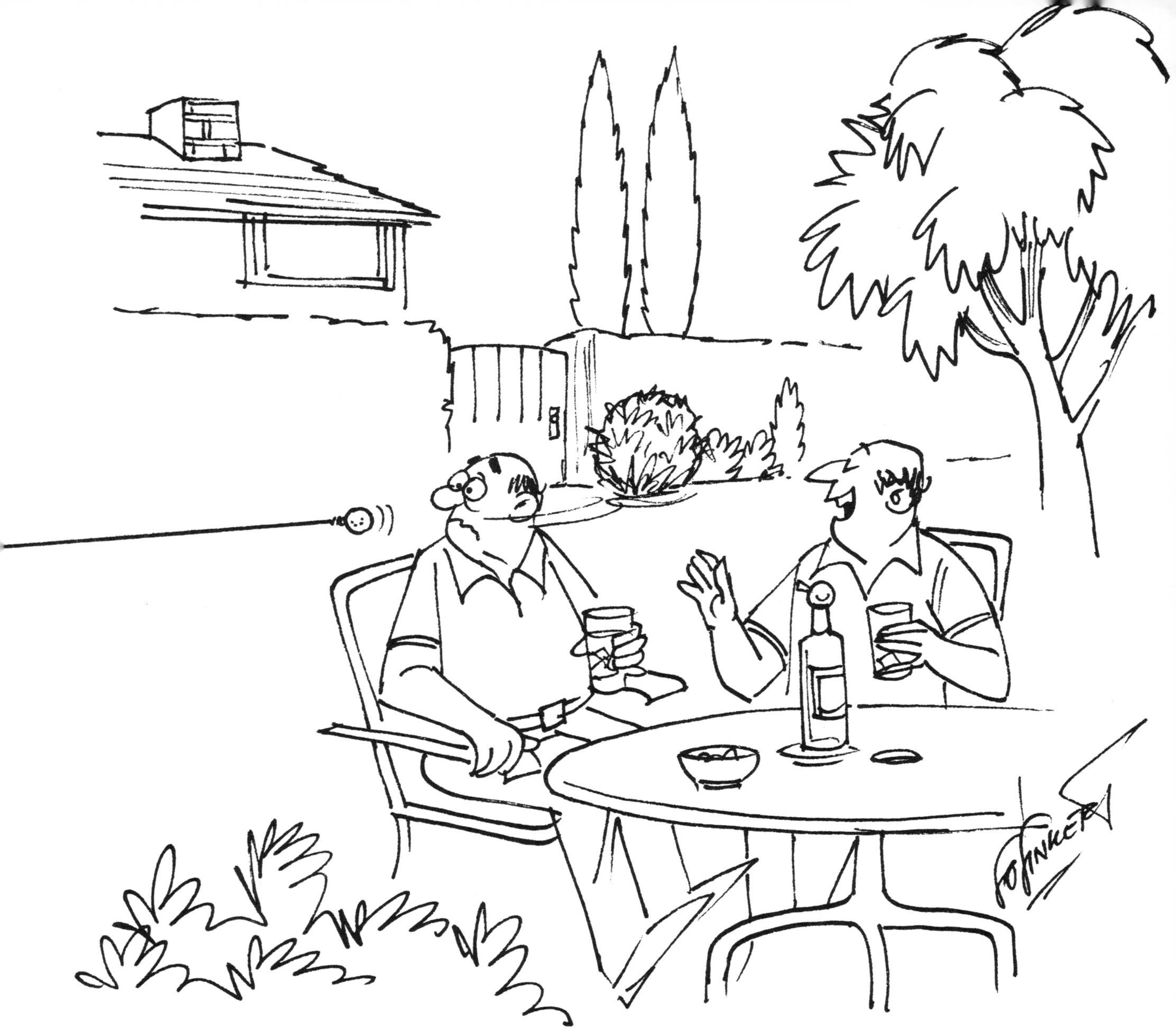

"DON'T LET THIS BOTHER YOU, THE NEIGHBOR IS PRACTICING WITH HIS GIZMO. THE BALL IS ATTACHED TO AN ELASTIC STRING."

"DAD, THE 19th HOLE EXPERT IS HERE!"

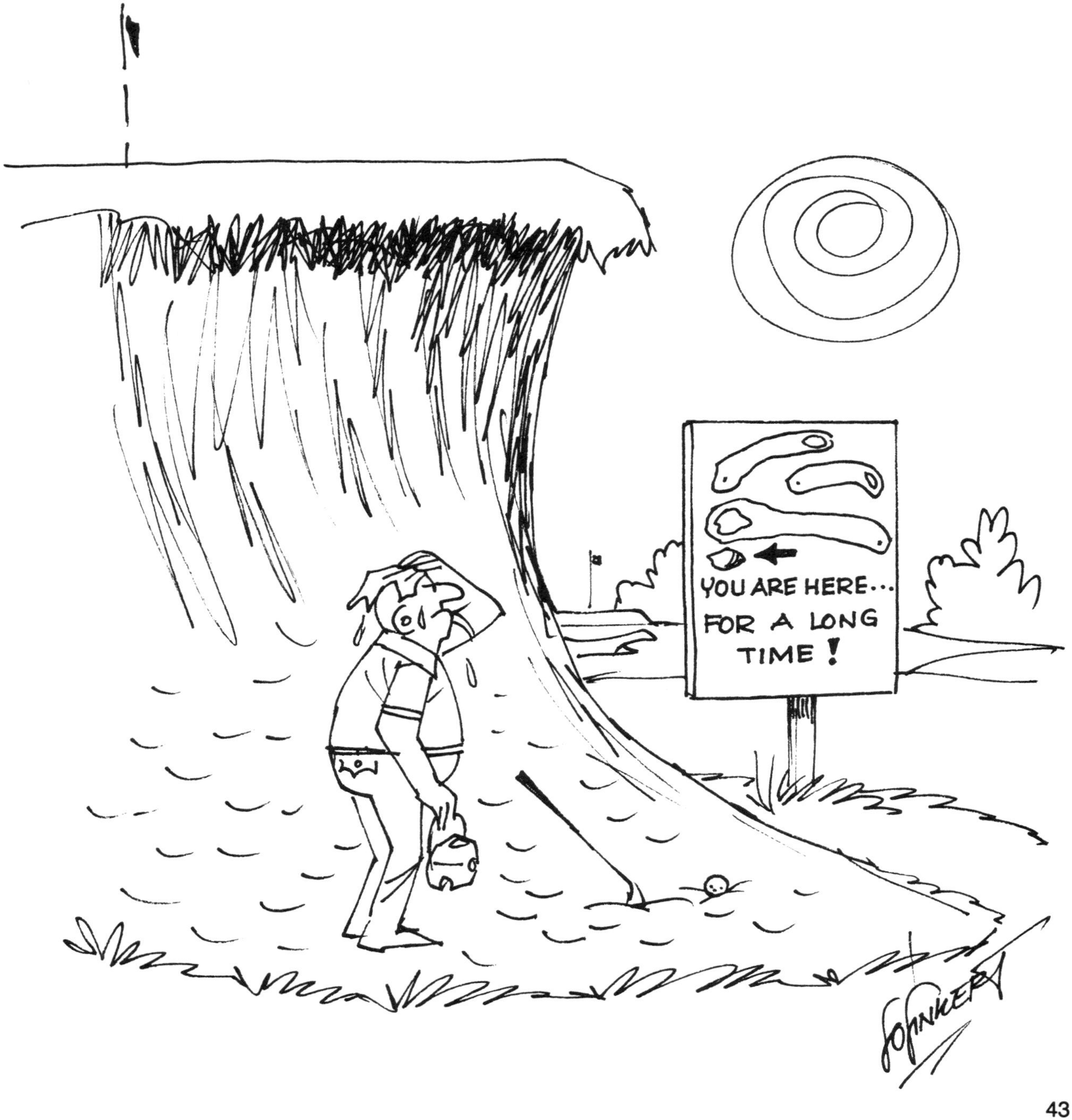
YOU ARE HERE...
FOR A LONG
TIME!

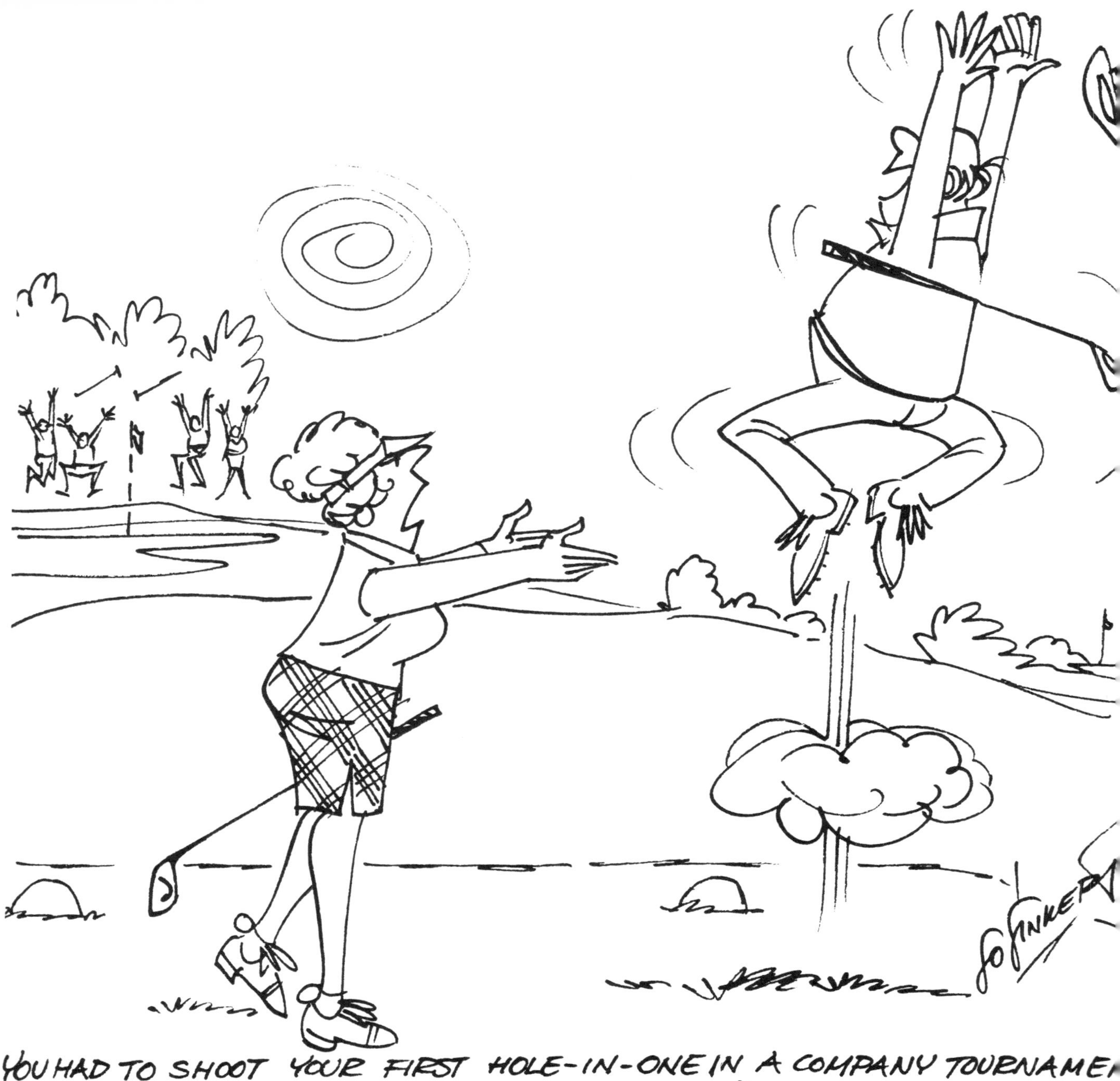

JO LINKER

"YOU HAD TO SHOOT YOUR FIRST HOLE-IN-ONE IN A COMPANY TOURNAME
WITH 150 PLAYERS AT $ 3.00 A DRINK IT WILL COST YOU $ 450.

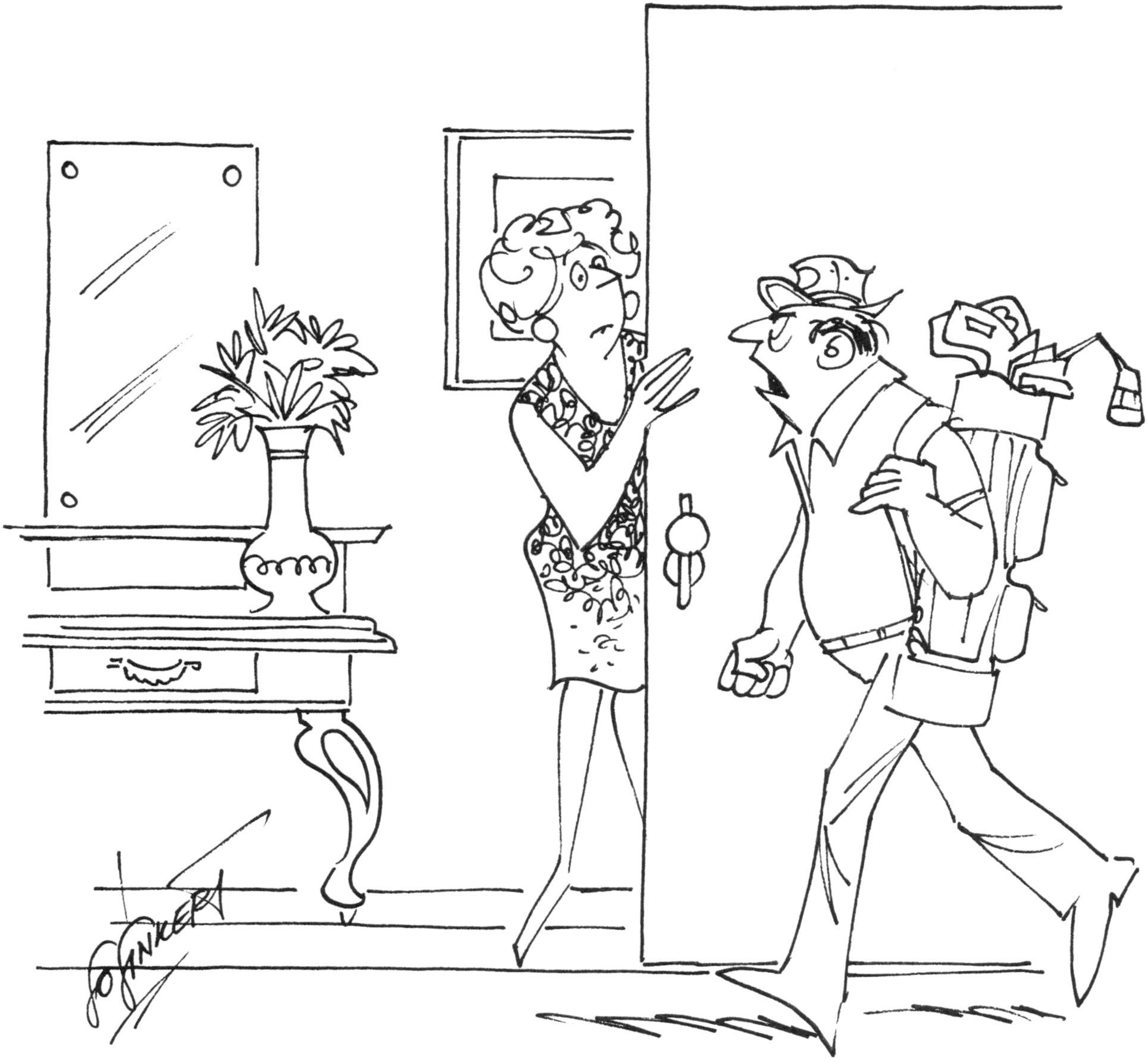

. . . AND HOW DID YOU BLOW YOUR DAY?"

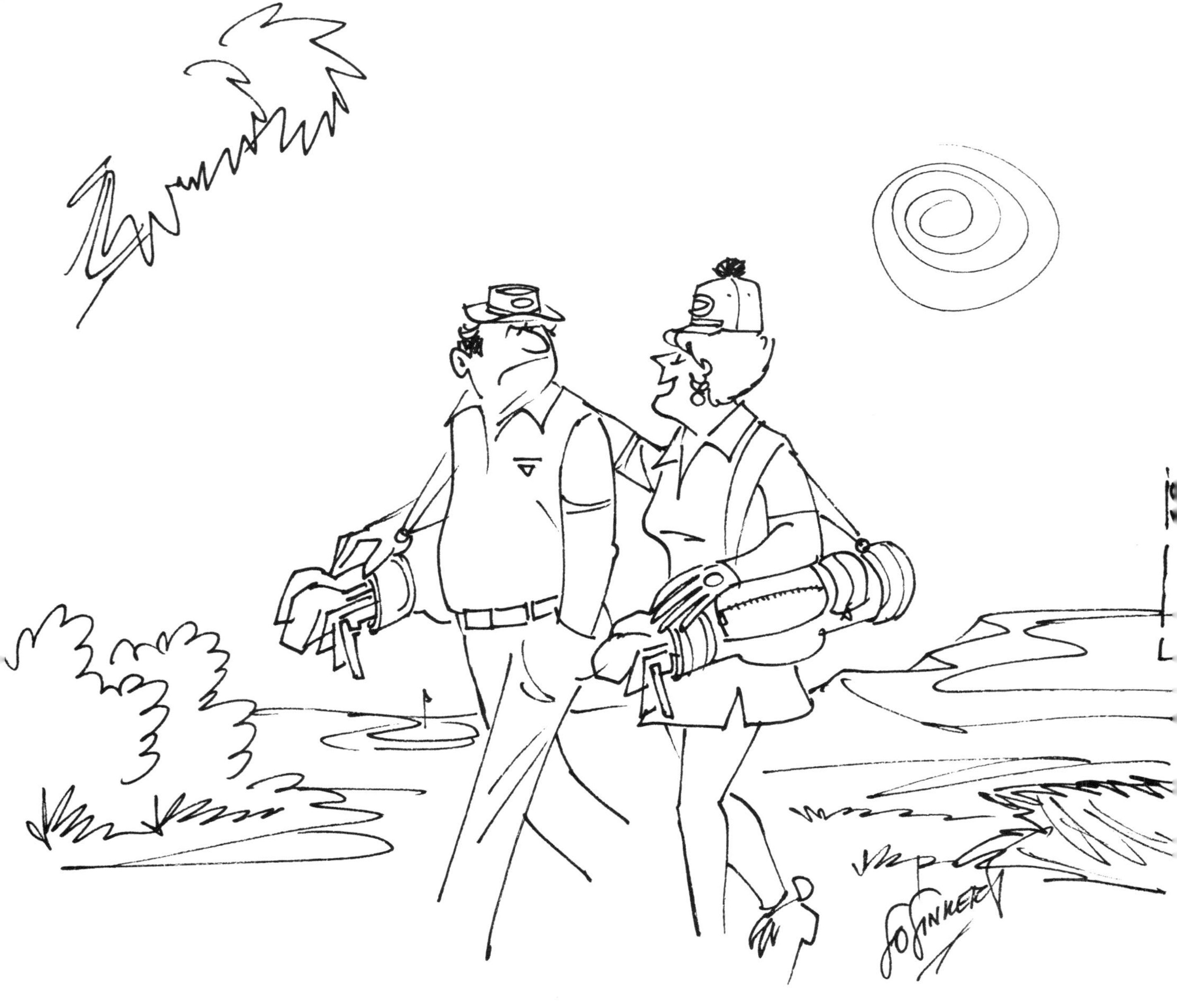
JO SINKER

"YOU'RE A GREAT GOLFER, A REAL CHAMP, A CLOSE GENIUS THAT'S WHY I'M SO HAPPY TO HAVE CLOBBERED YOU."

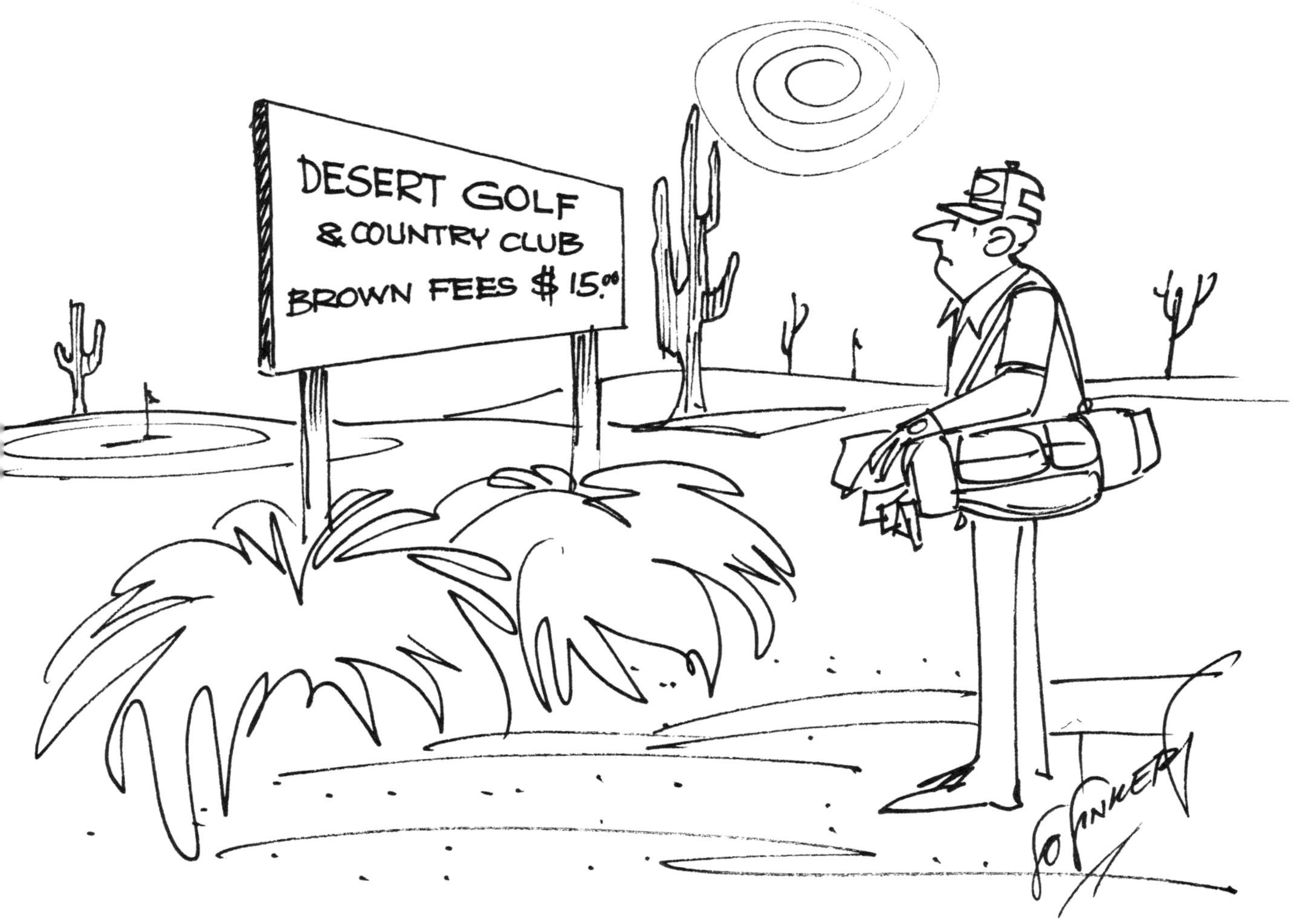
DESERT GOLF
& COUNTRY CLUB
BROWN FEES $ 15.00

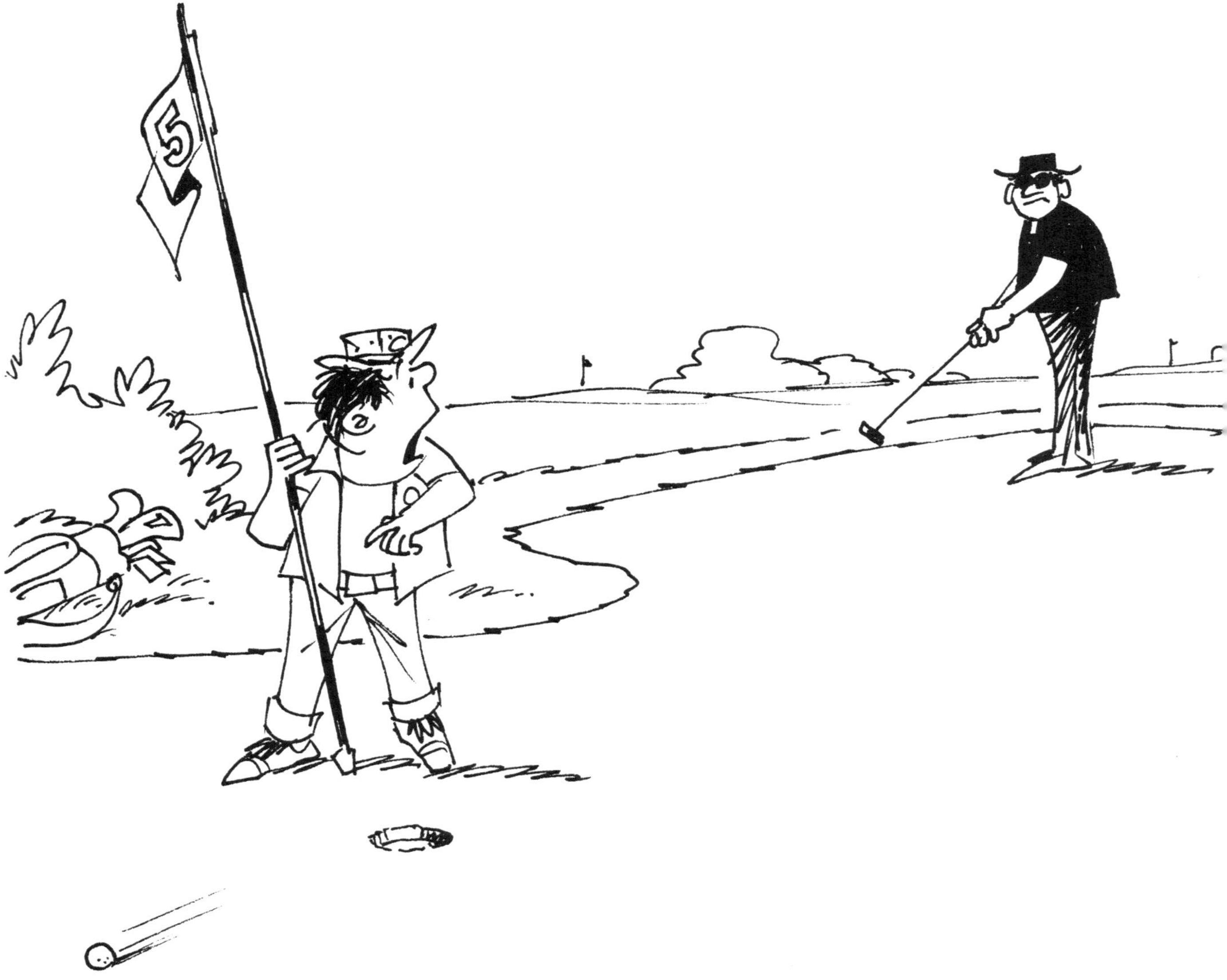

"FATHER, YOUR BALL RUNNETH OVER!"

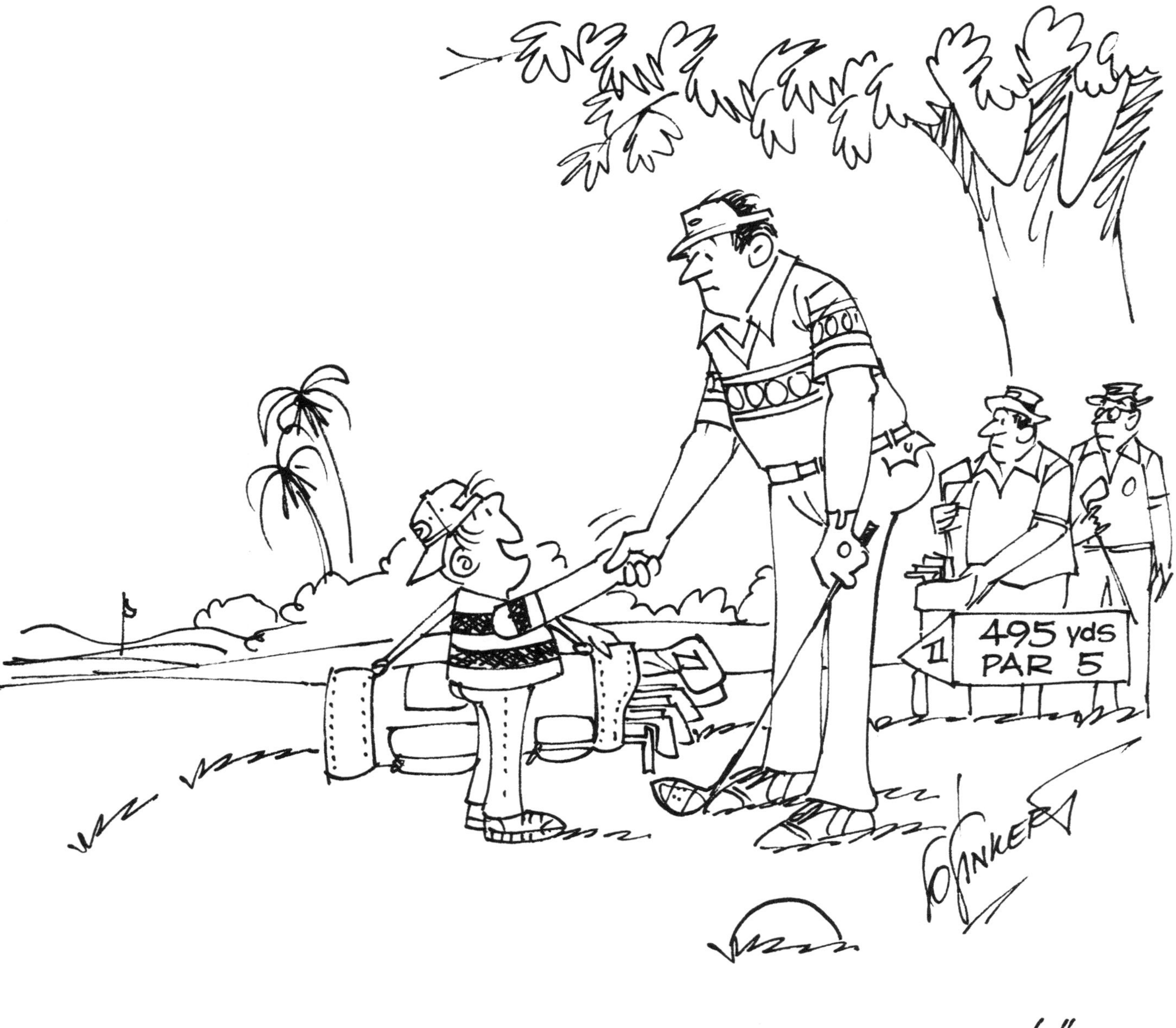
495 yds
PAR 5
1

" I JUST GOT THIS JOB HOPING TO MEET YOU...DAD! "

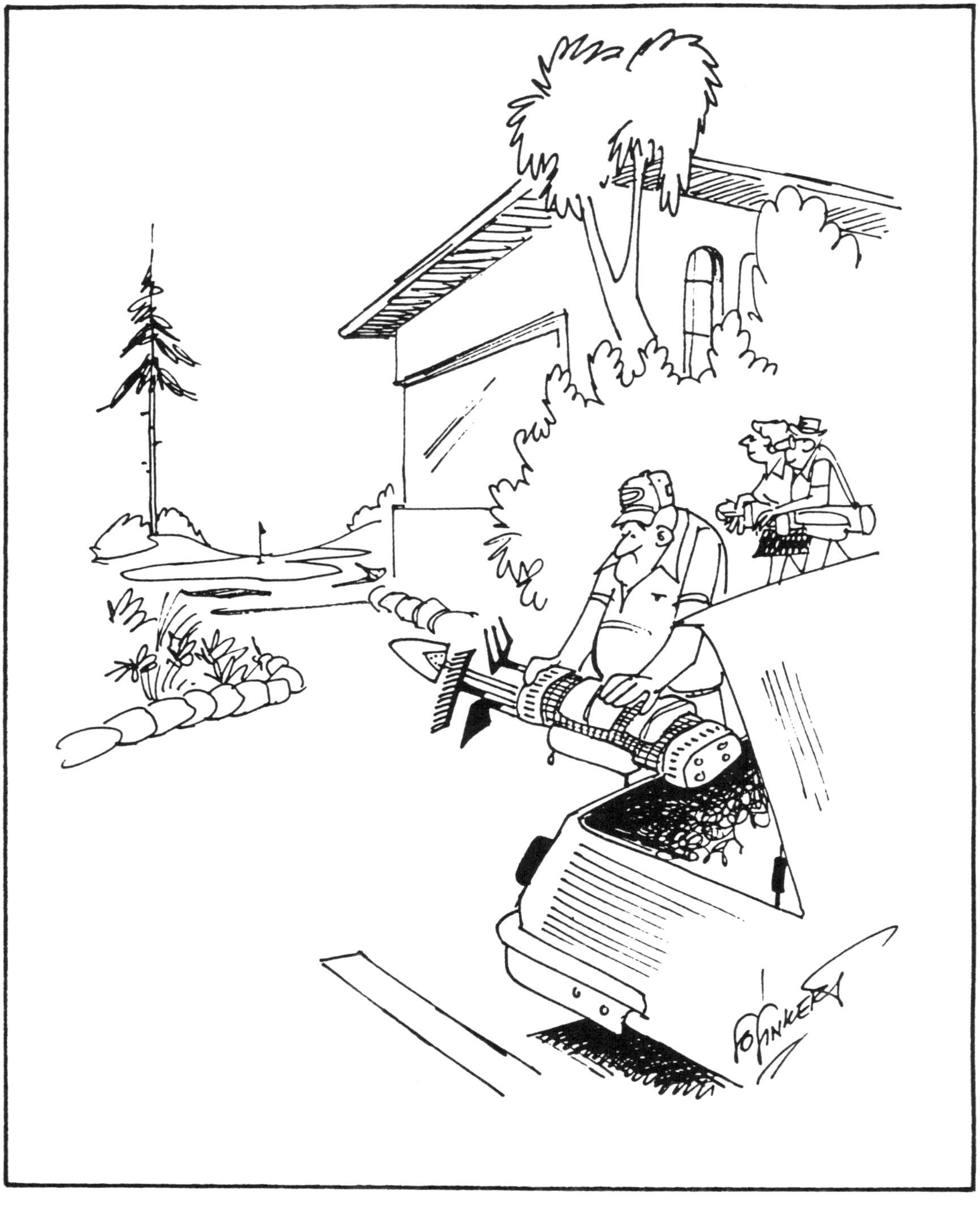

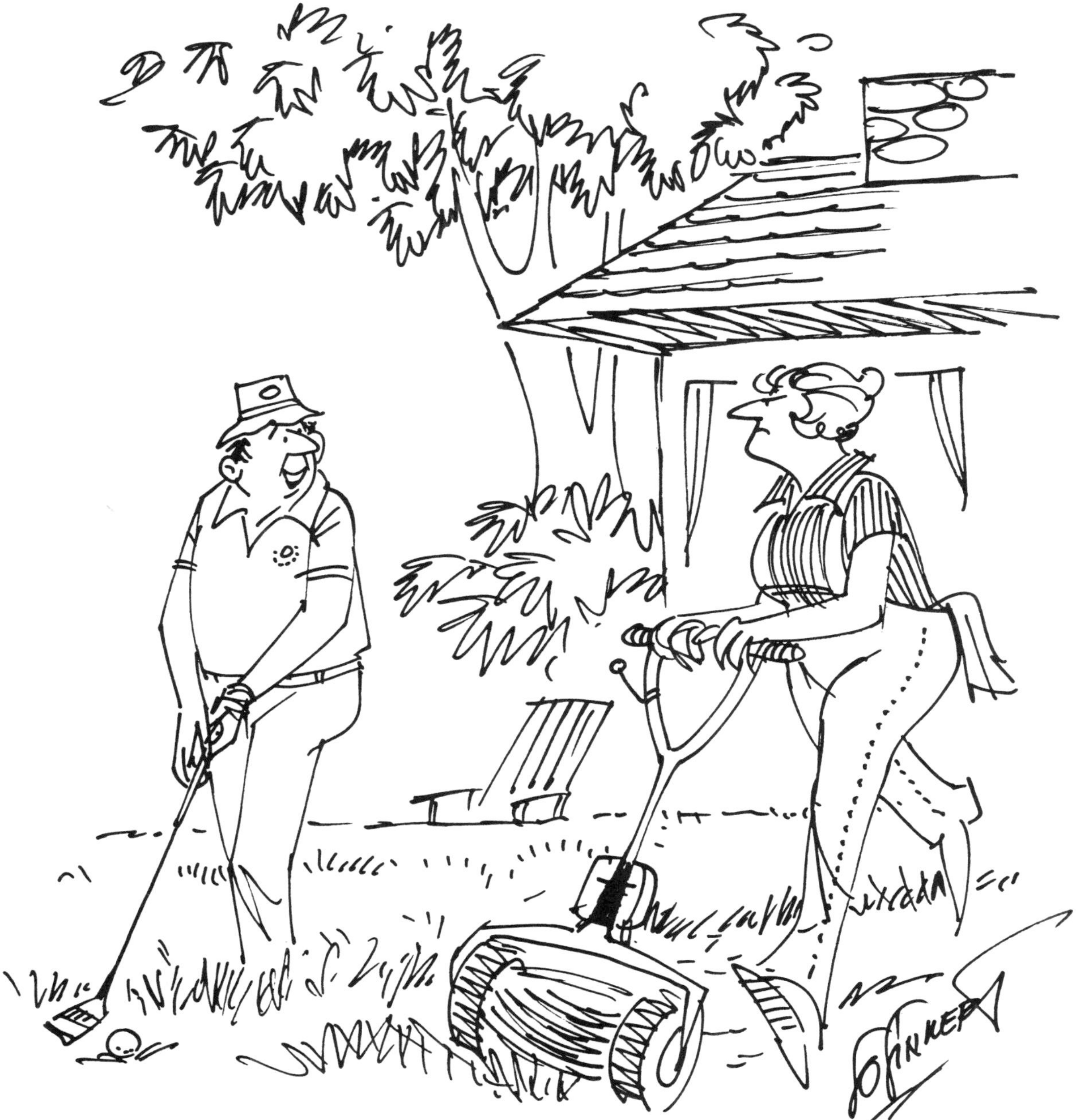

"DO YOU MIND IF I PLAY THROUGH, ELIZABETH?

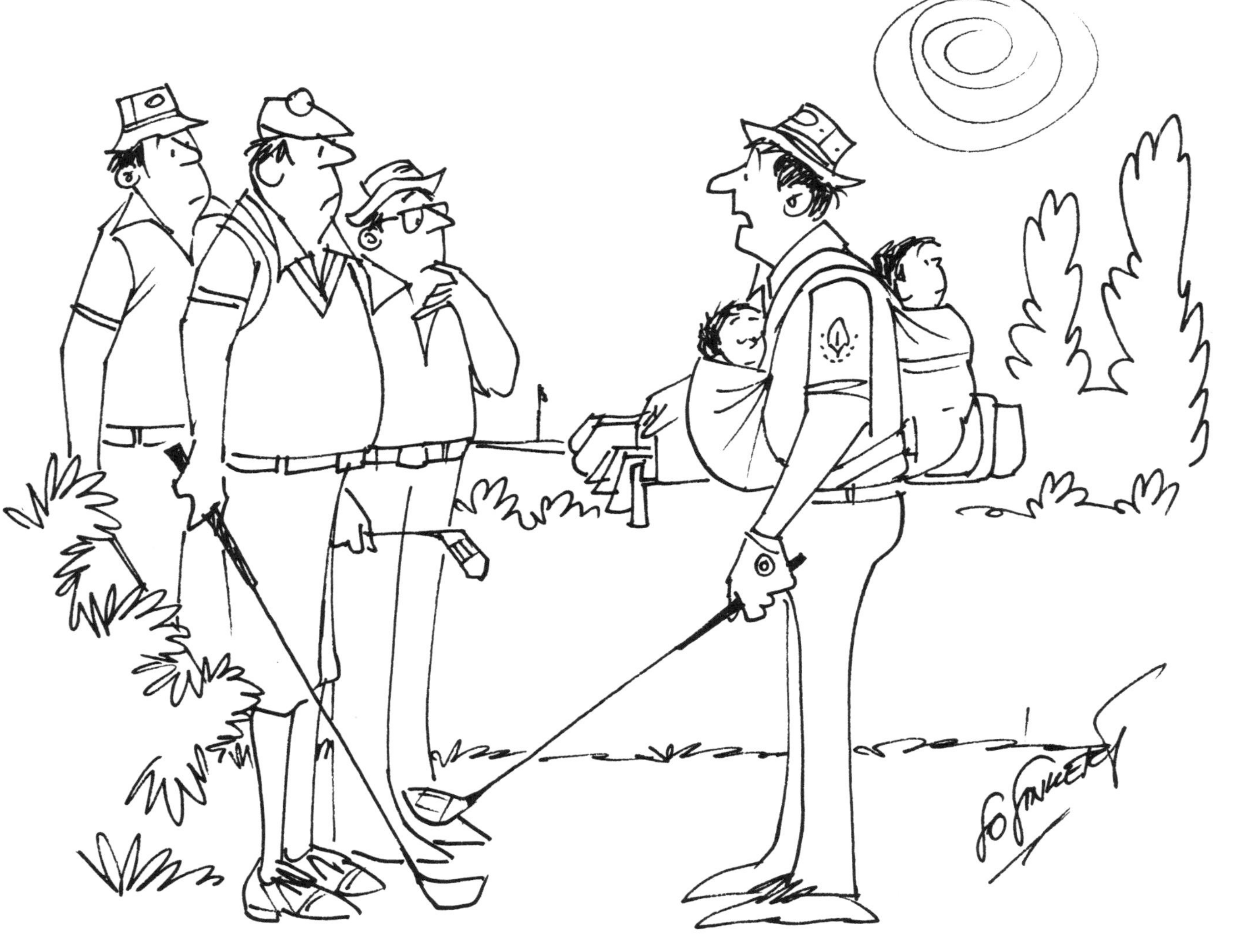

" MY WIFE HAD TO GO TO WORK AND THE BABYSITTER GOT SICK."

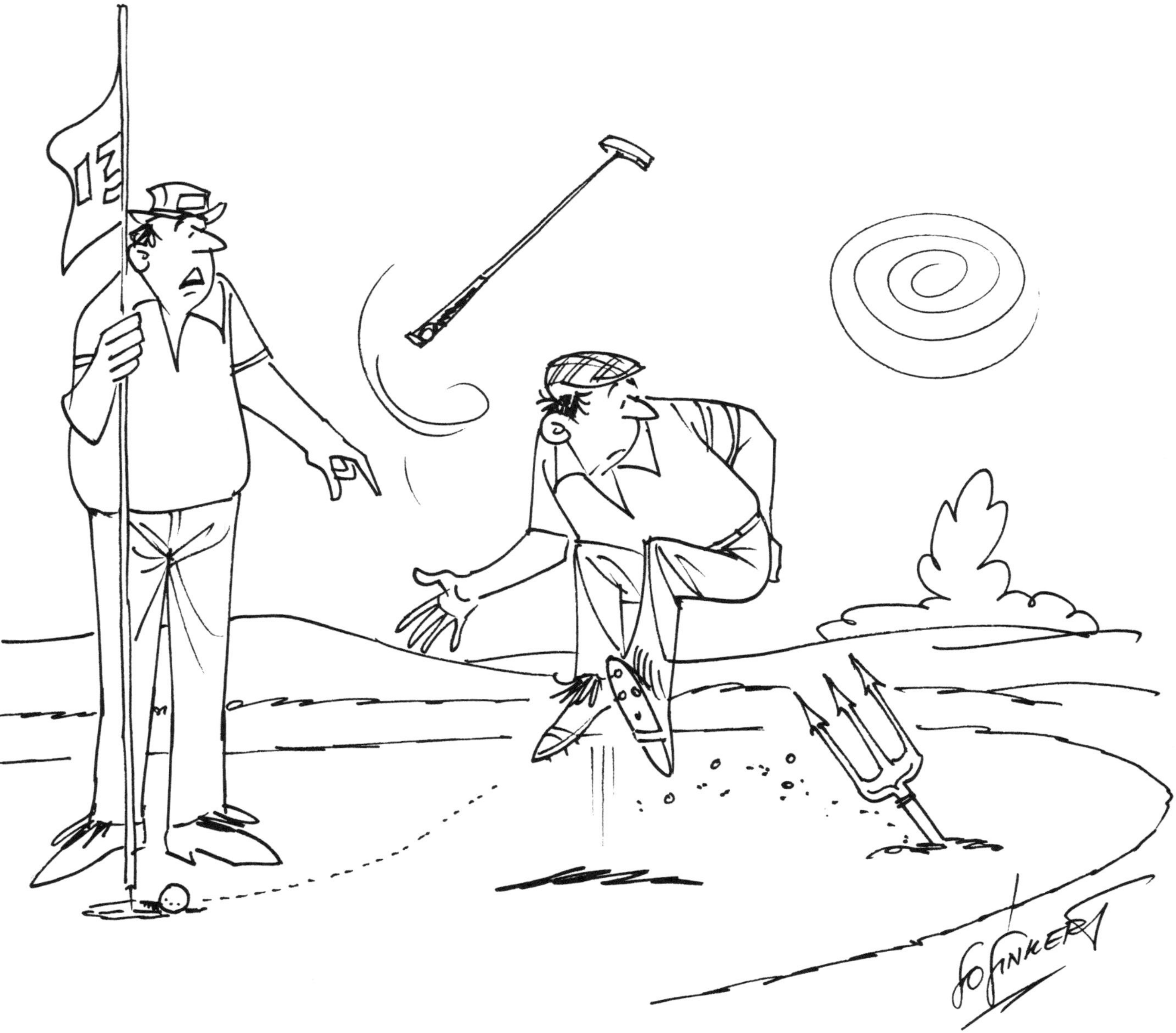

"SOMEBODY DOWN THERE DOESN'T LIKE YOU!"

"I DON'T THINK IT'S FAIR TO HAVE THE ROUGH RIGHT NEXT TO THE FAIRWAY!"

"...AND WILL YOU, MATHILDE, LEARN TO PLAY GOLF OR FIND SOMETHING TO BUSY YOURSELF WHEN CHARLES IS OUT ON THE COURSE?"

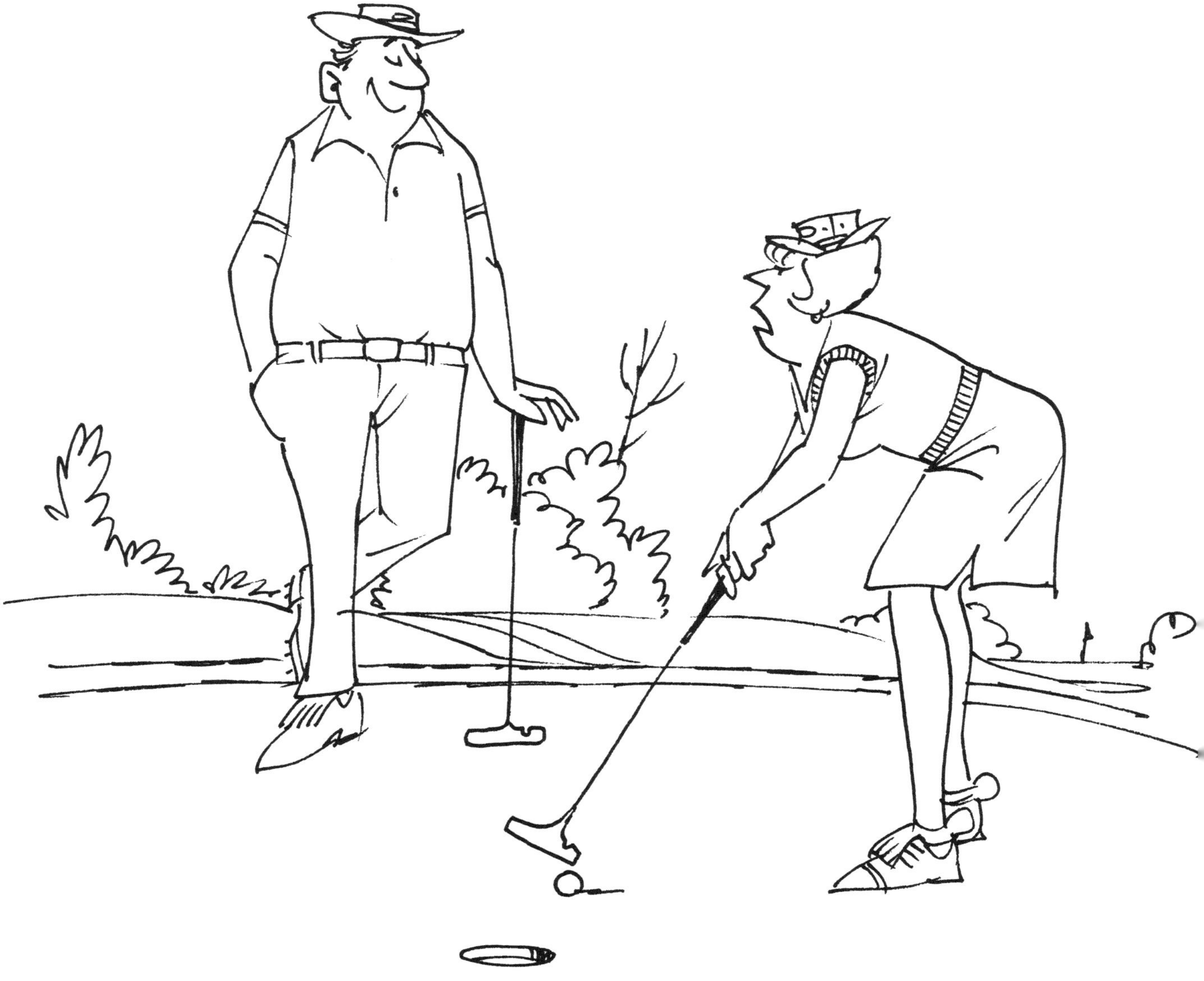

" WHAT EVER HAPPENS TO THIS PUTT, PLEASE DON'T SAY AGAIN YOU MISSED IT BY A SILLY LITTLE MILLIMETER! "

"LIKE THE WAY I IMPROVED YOUR GRIP WITH CRAZY GLUE?"

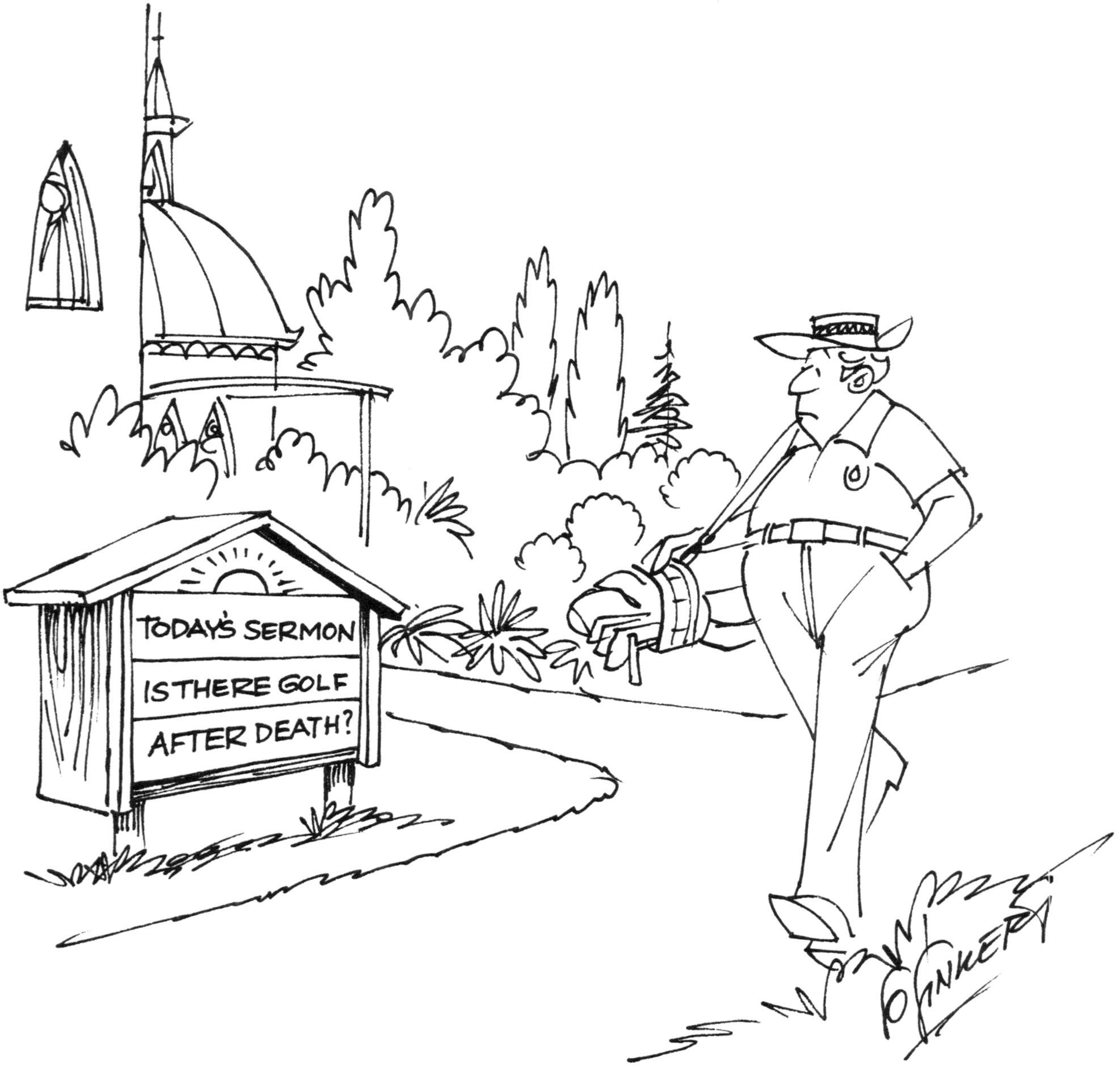
TODAY'S SERMON
IS THERE GOLF
AFTER DEATH?
PINKERT

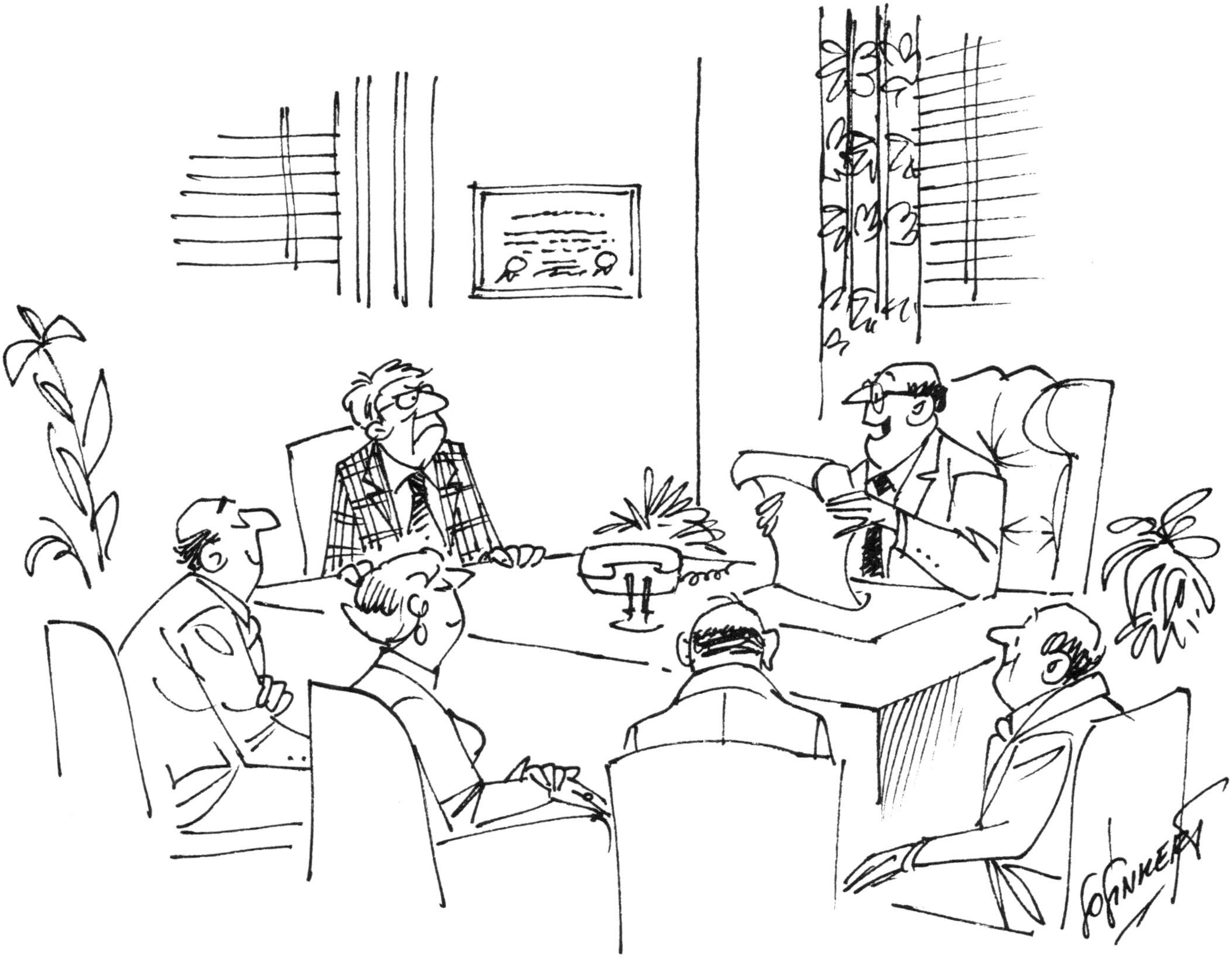
SOPINKER

"...AND TO MY NEPHEW RAY, WHO NEVER BROKE A HUNDRED I LEAVE MY EIGHT HANDICAP AT THE MISSION GOLF & COUNTRY CLUB."

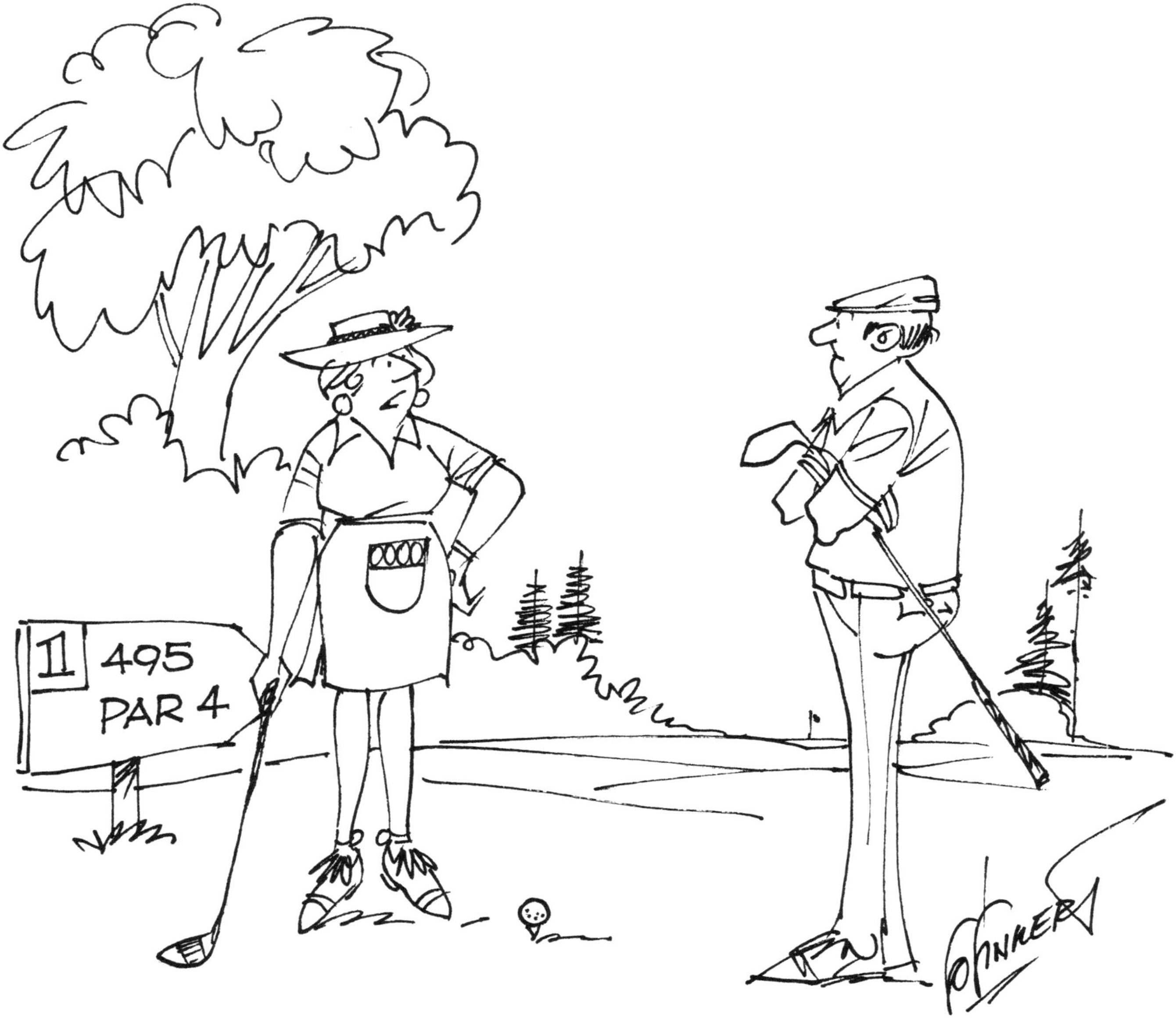
1
495
PAR 4

"OK, WHERE'S THE GOAL?"

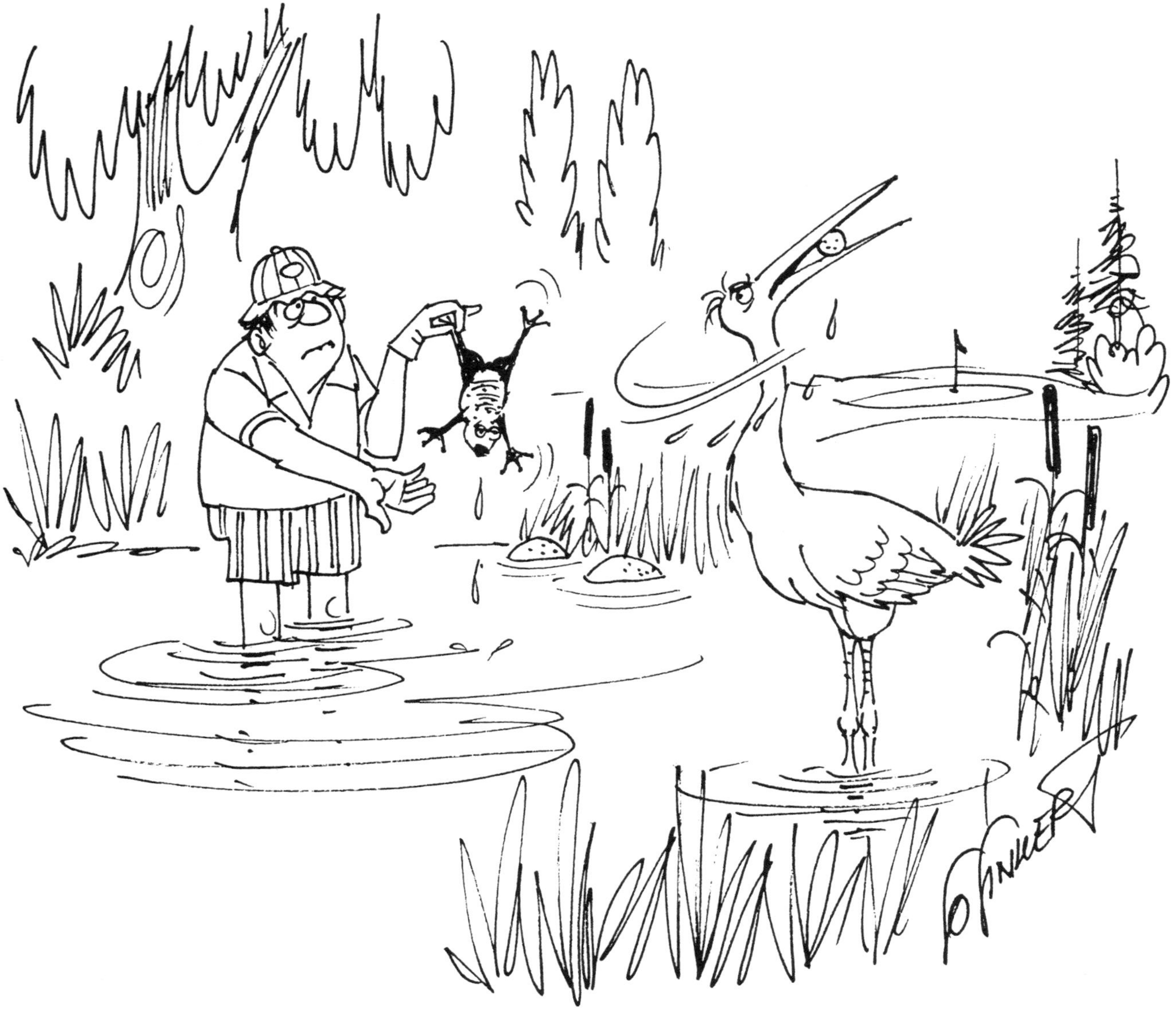

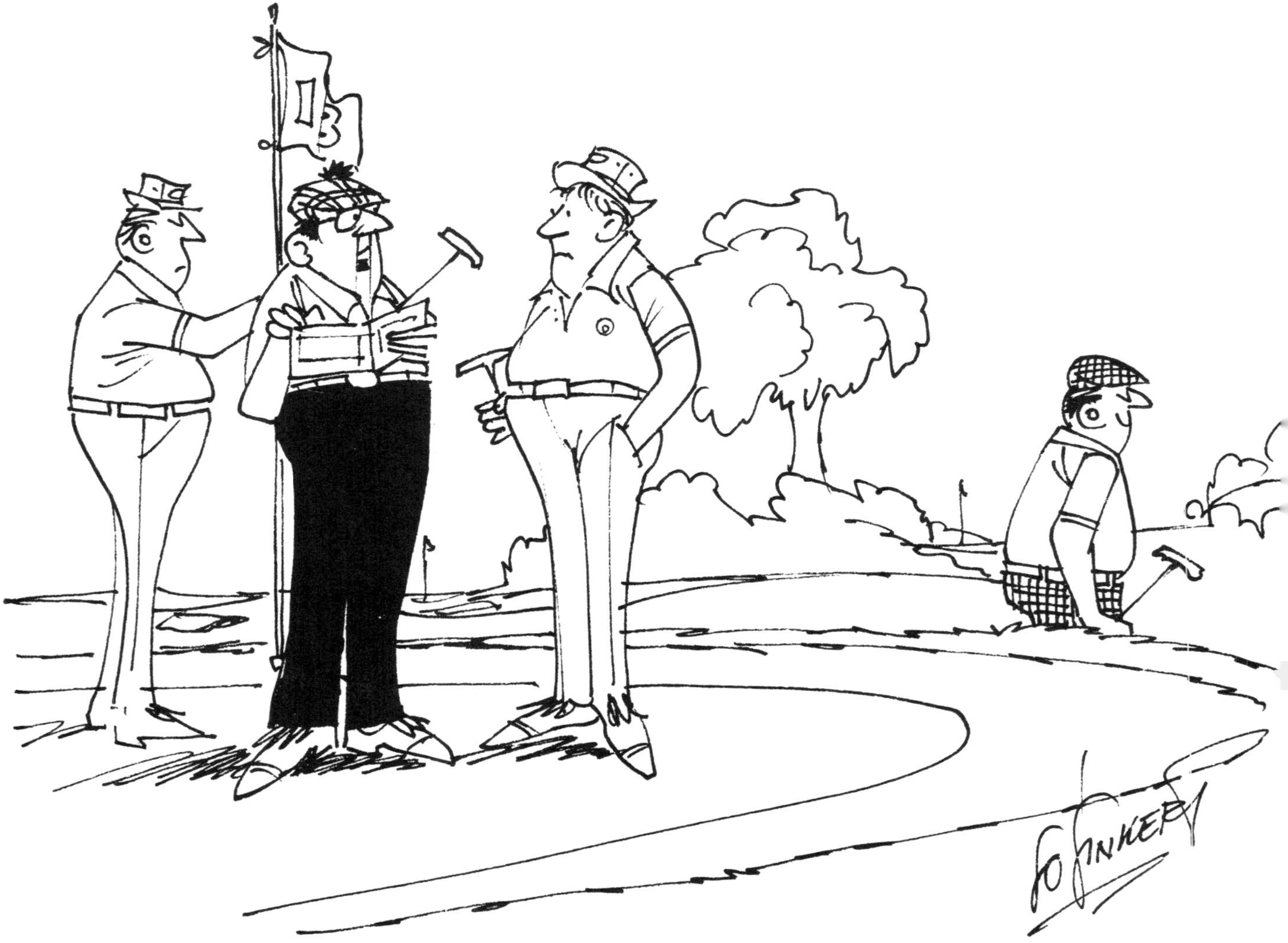
13

"HE PLAYS GOLF LIKE A POLITICIAN, HE LIES AND SMILES AT THE SAME TIME."

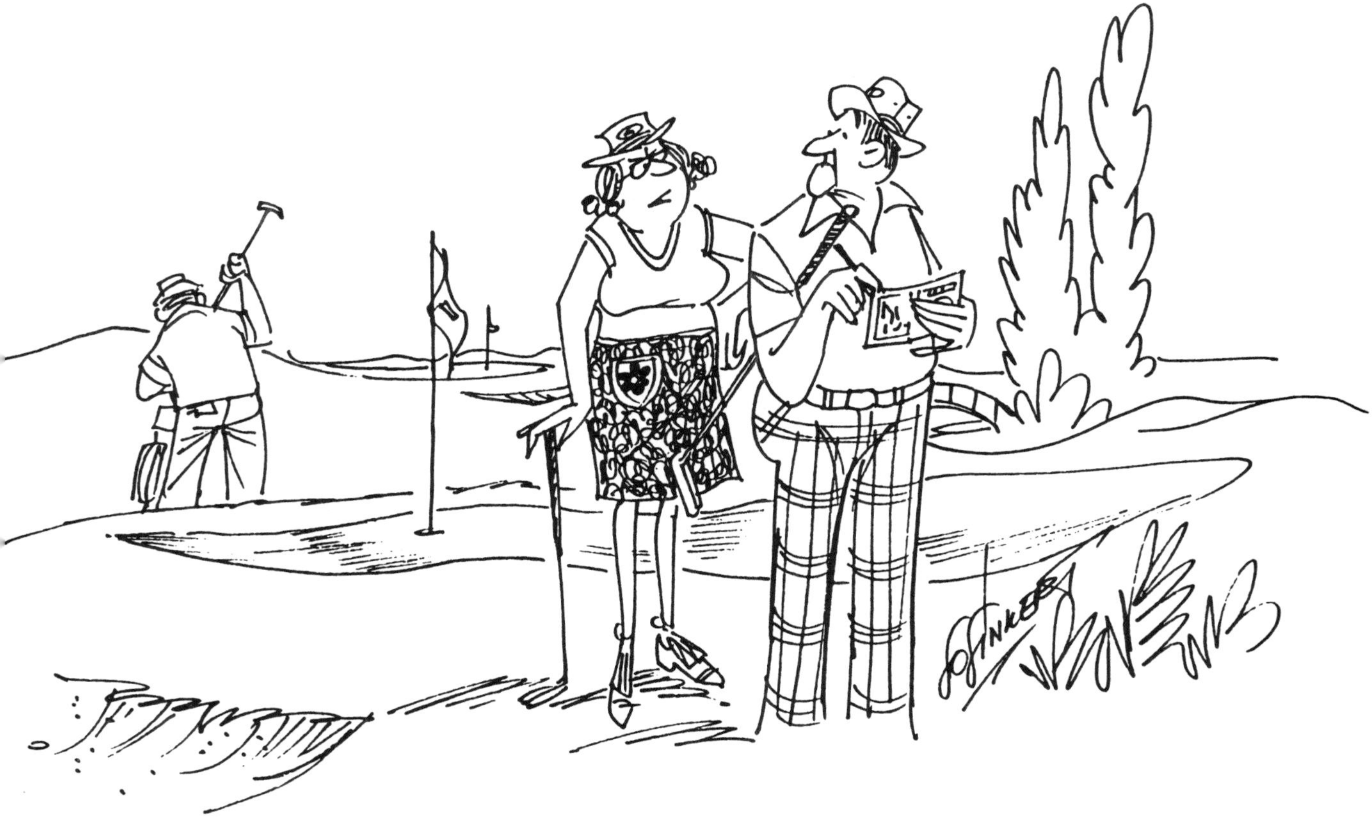

"I WISH YOU'D STOP TELLING PEOPLE I'M WHAT'S THE MATTER WITH YOUR GAME."

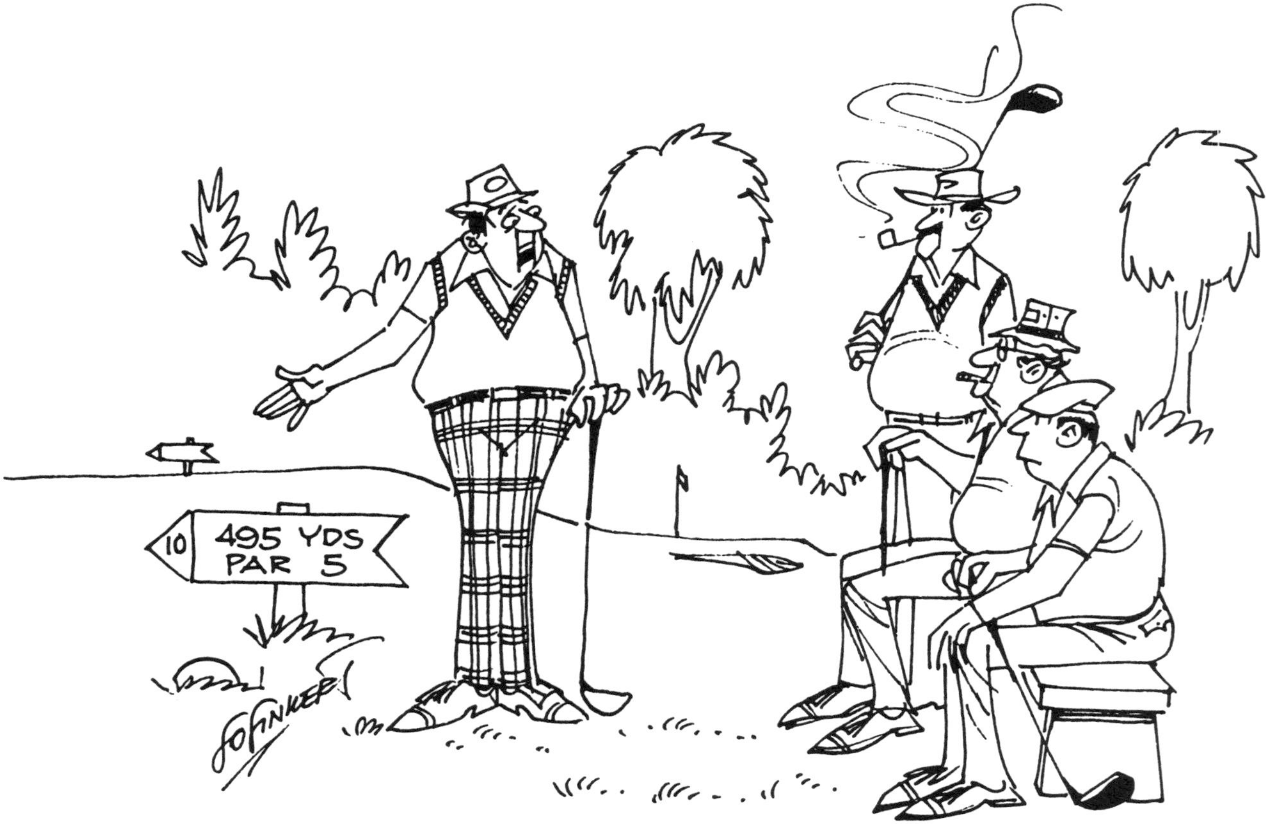
10
495 YDS
PAR 5

"OKAY, LOW MAN UP...

WHO HAD LESS THAN A 9 ON THE LAST HOLE?"

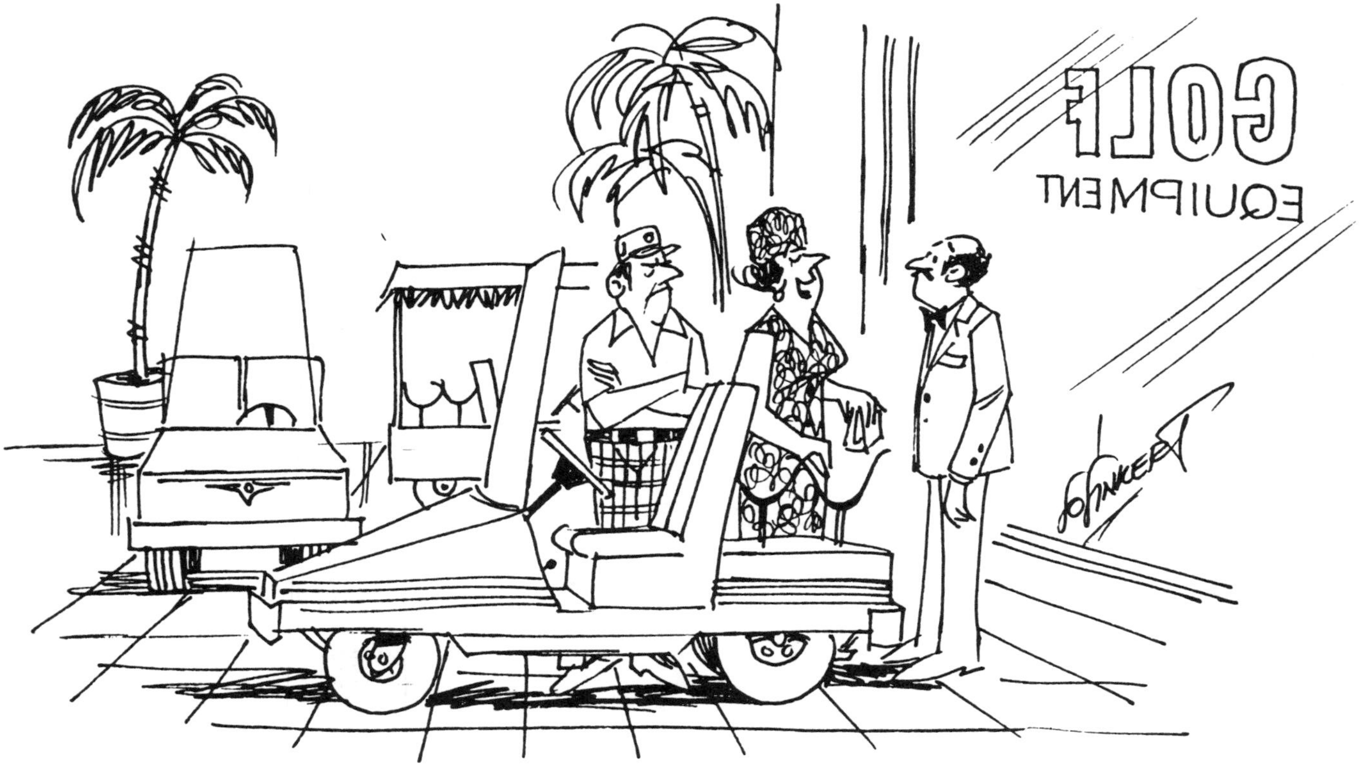
GOLF
EQUIPMENT

"WE'LL BUY IT -- IF IT COMES WITH A LAWNMOWER ATTACHMENT."

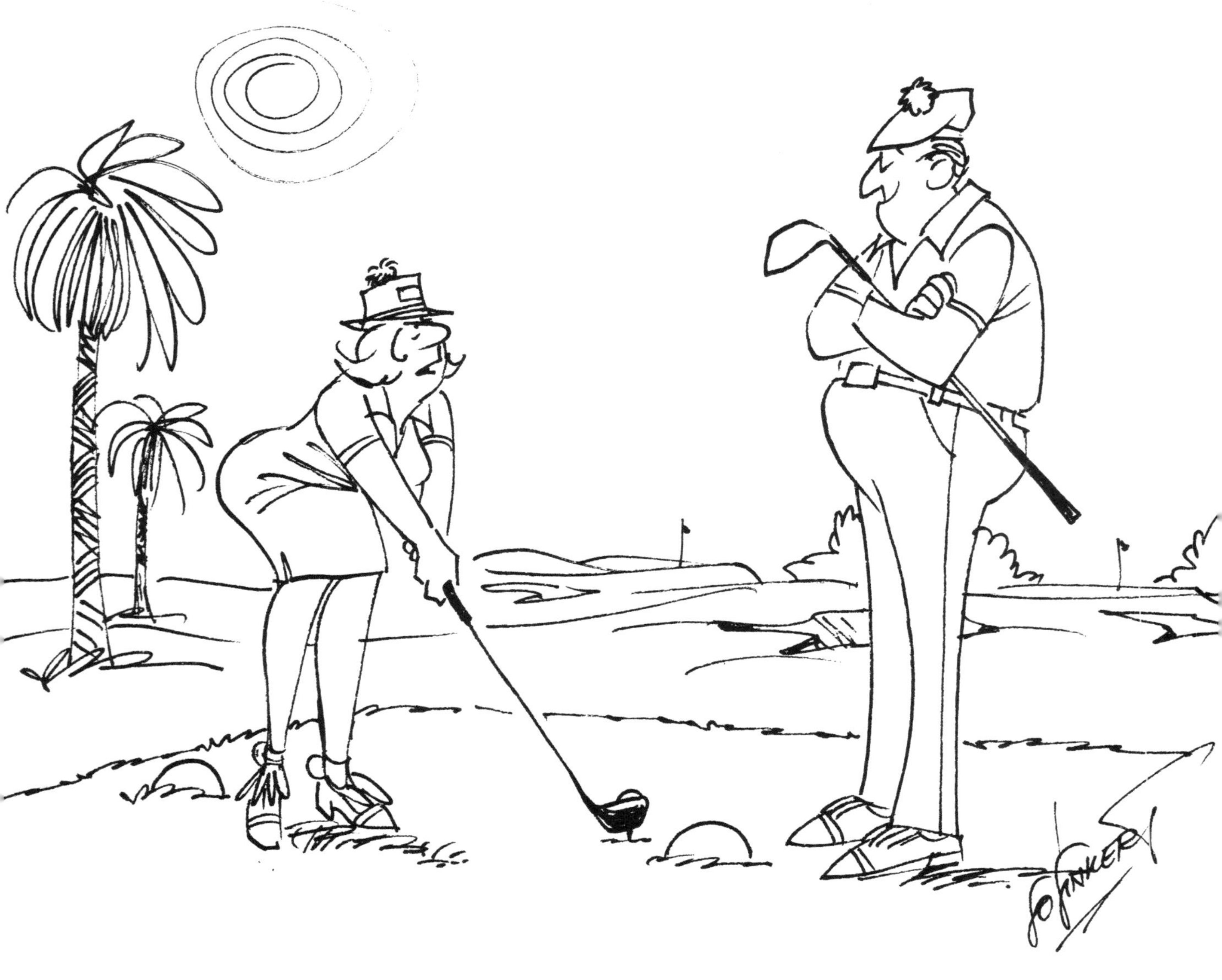

"REMEMBER, WHATEVER HAPPENS, NO WISE CRACKS LIKE A HIT AND A MISS!"

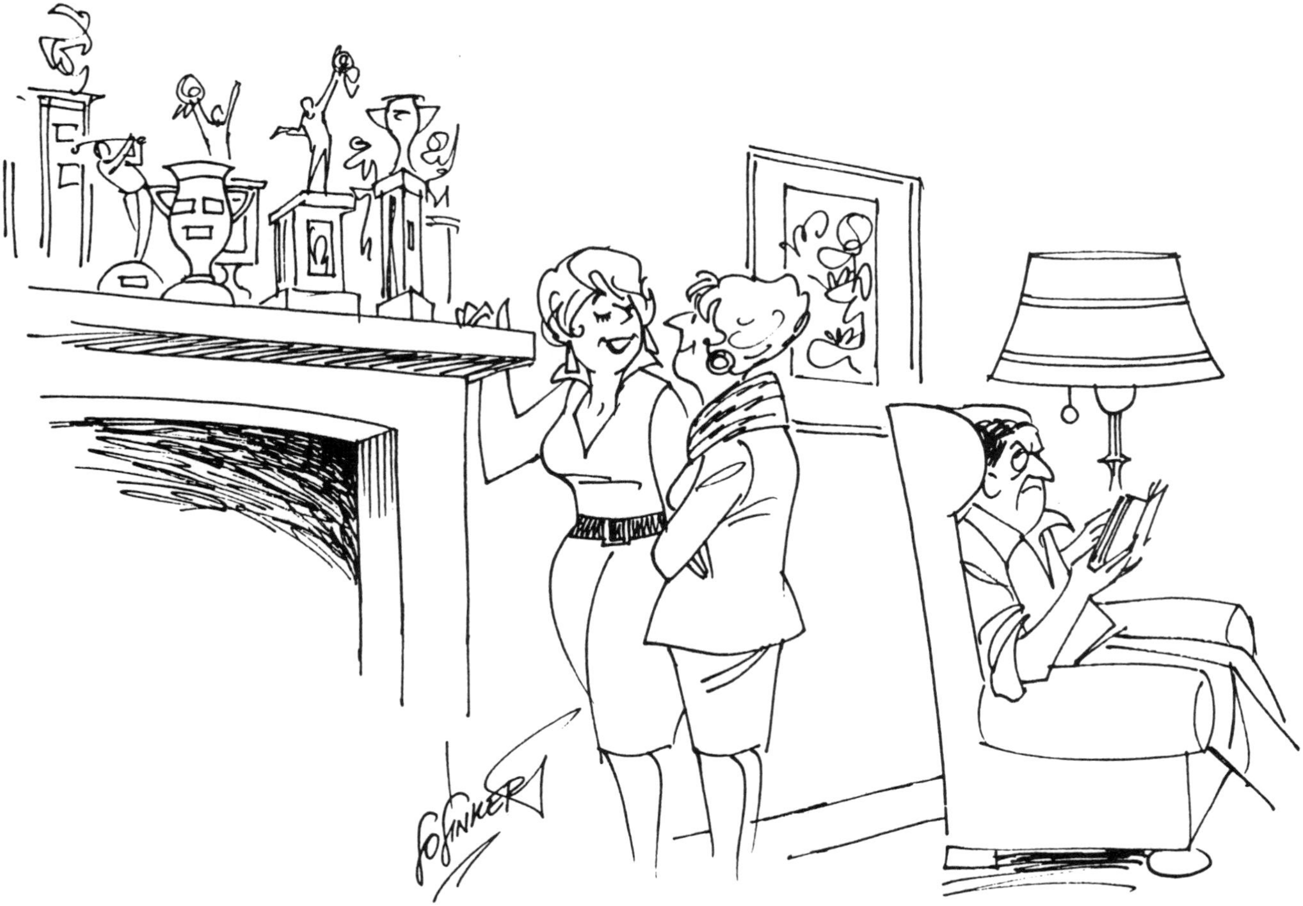

"HAROLD HAD A NO-HITTER ONCE –
UNFORTUNATELY IT WAS ON THE GOLF COURSE!"

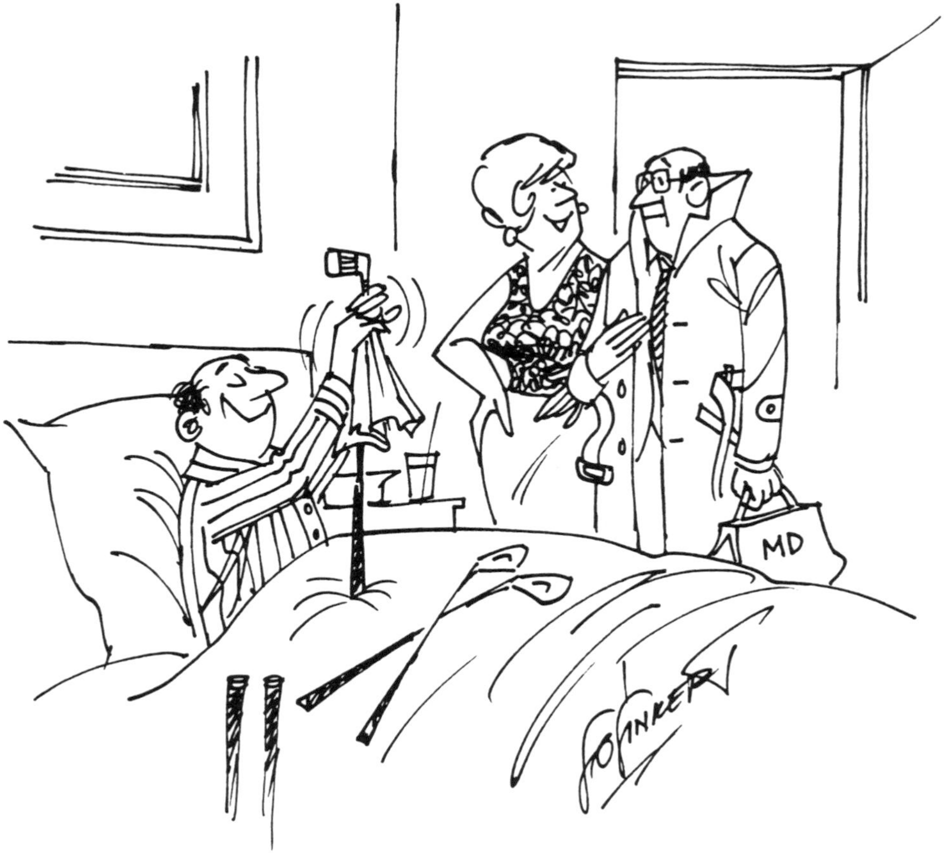
MD

"HE'S FEELING MORE UP TO PAR TODAY, DOCTOR."

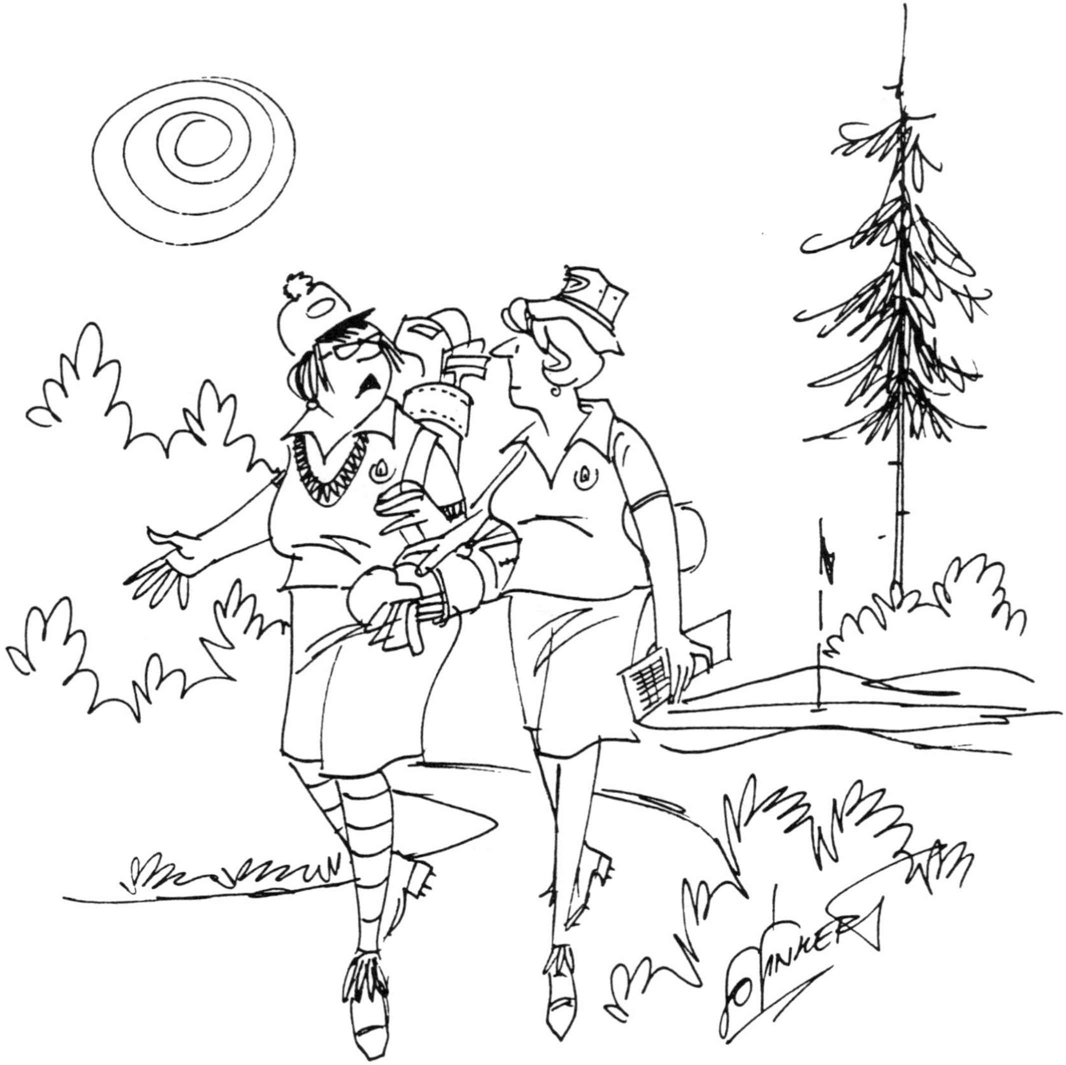

"FOR AWHILE I WAS THREE PUTTING ALMOST EVERY GREEN, BUT THEN I LOST MY TOUCH."

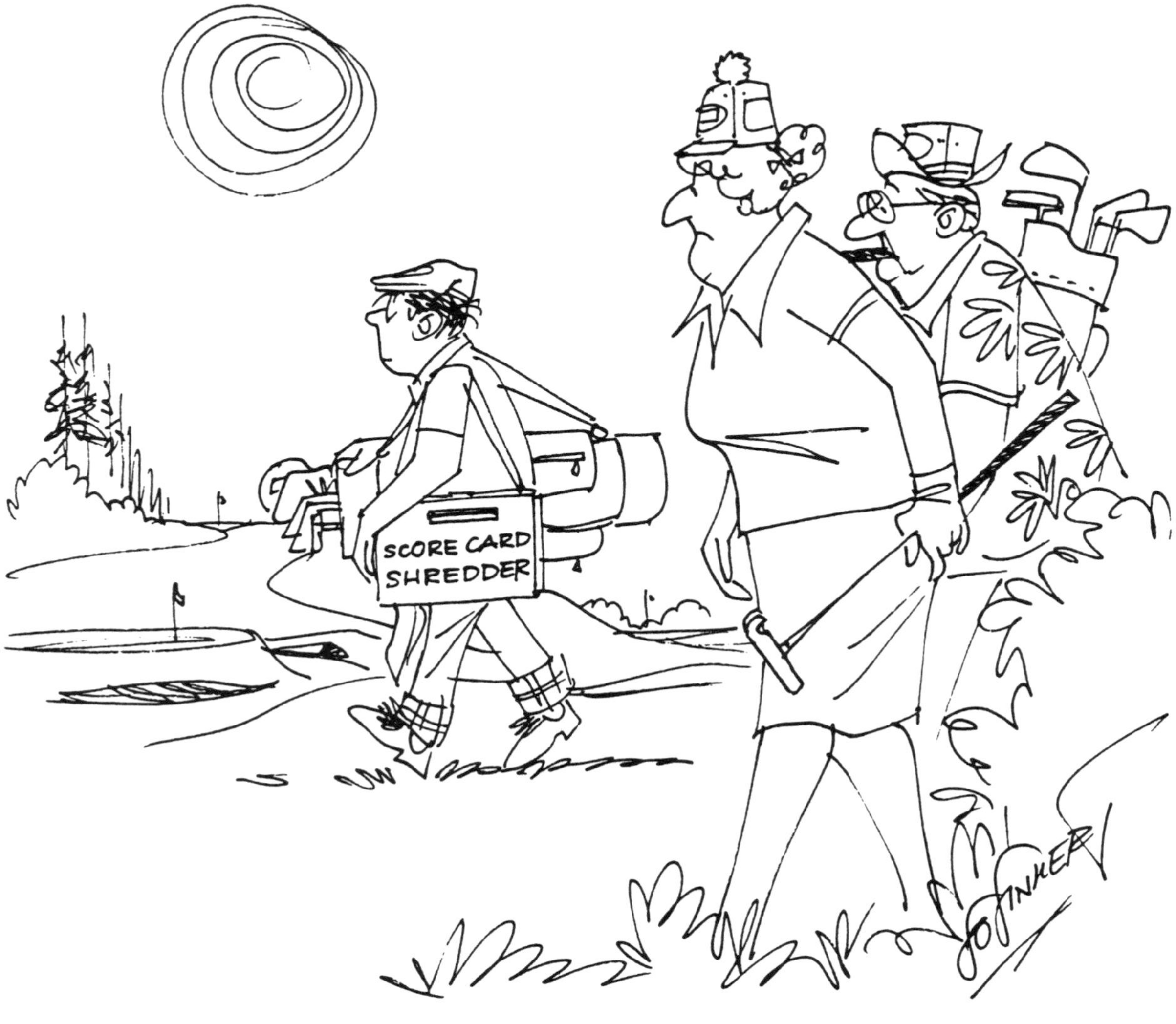
SCORE CARD
SHREDDER
JO TINKER

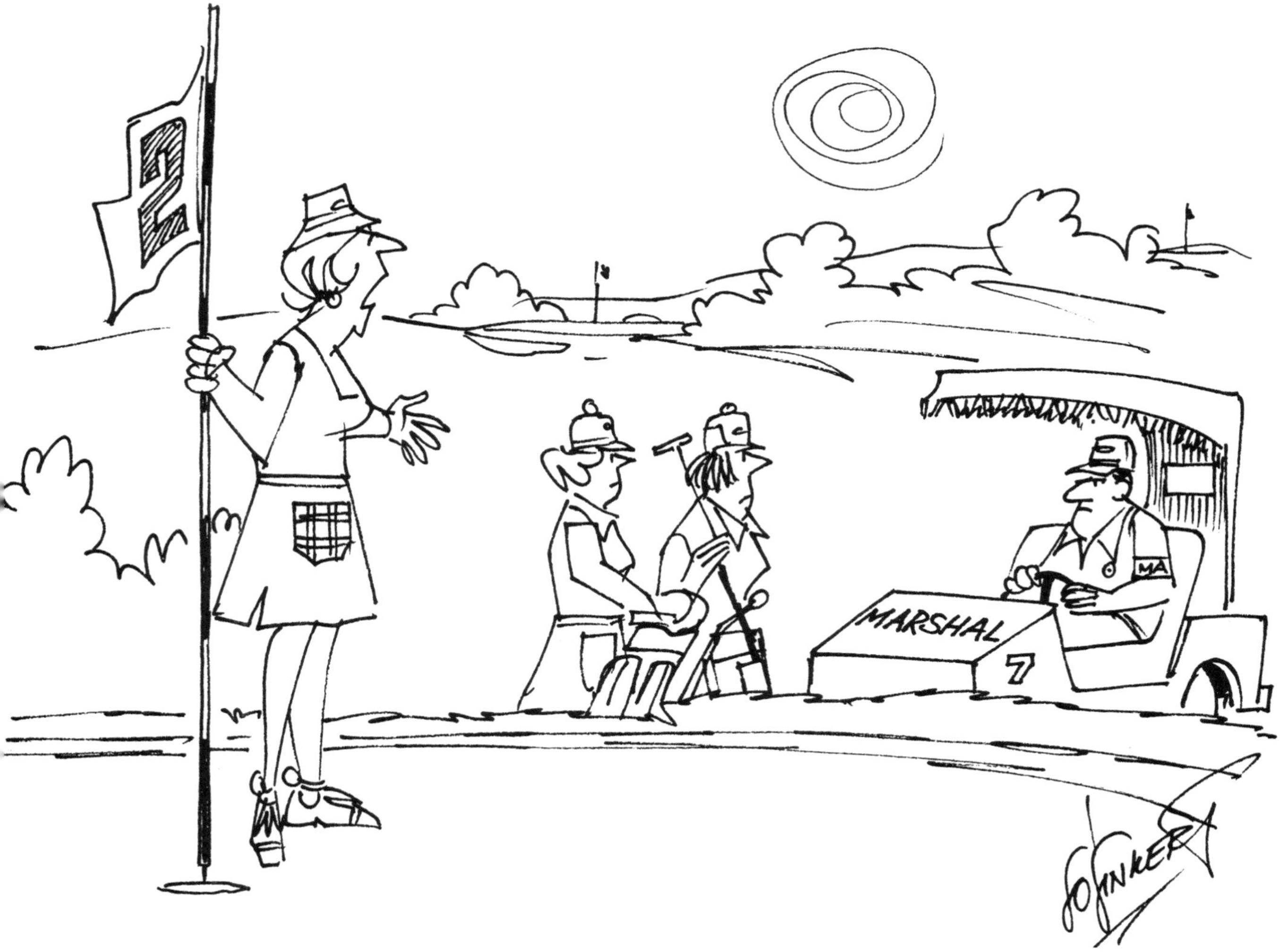
2
MARSHAL
7
MA

HOW CAN WE BE 3 HOLES BEHIND IF WE'RE ONLY PLAYING ON THE SECOND HOLE ?"

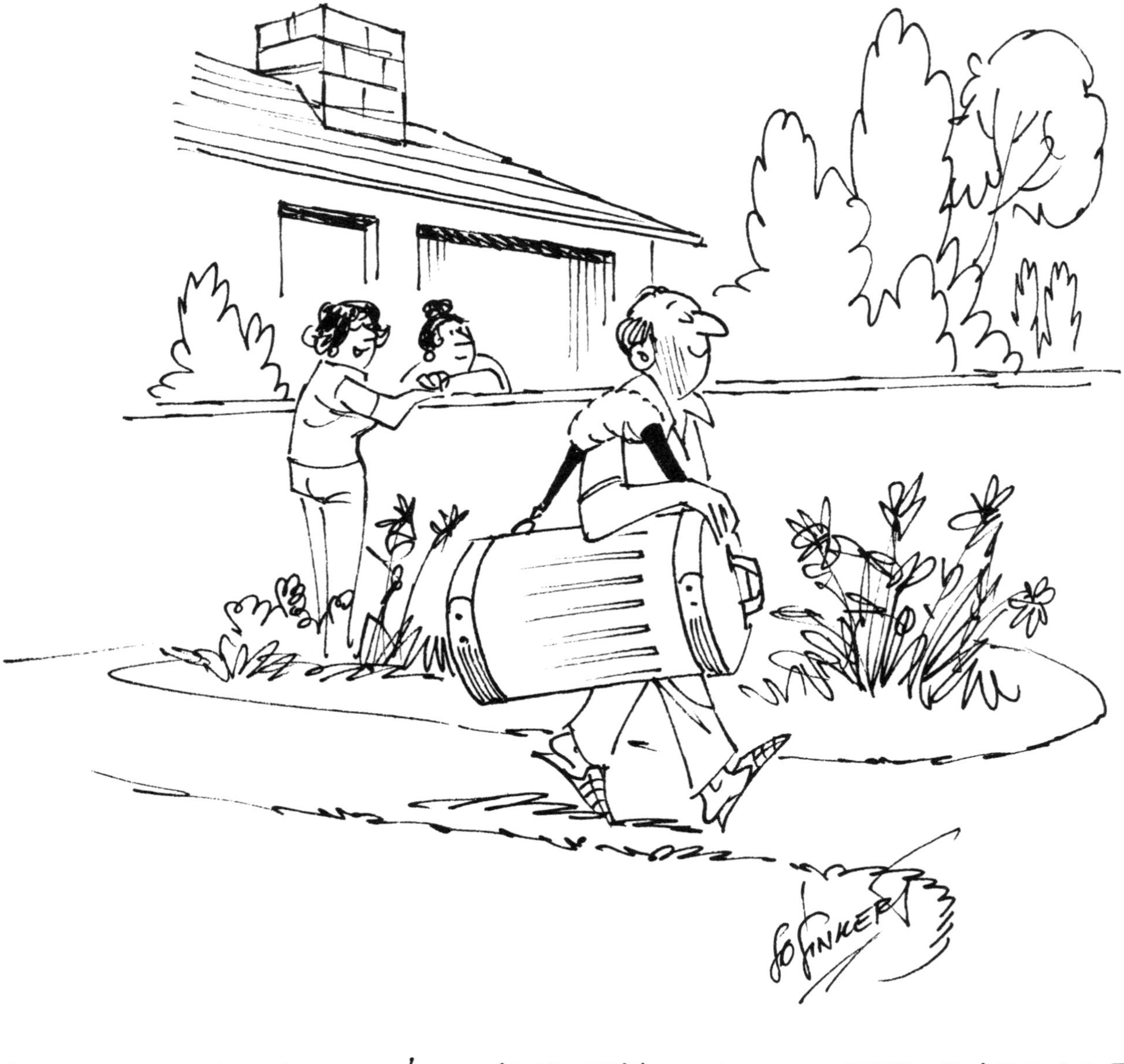

" THAT WAY HE DOESN'T MIND TAKING OUT THE GARBAGE."

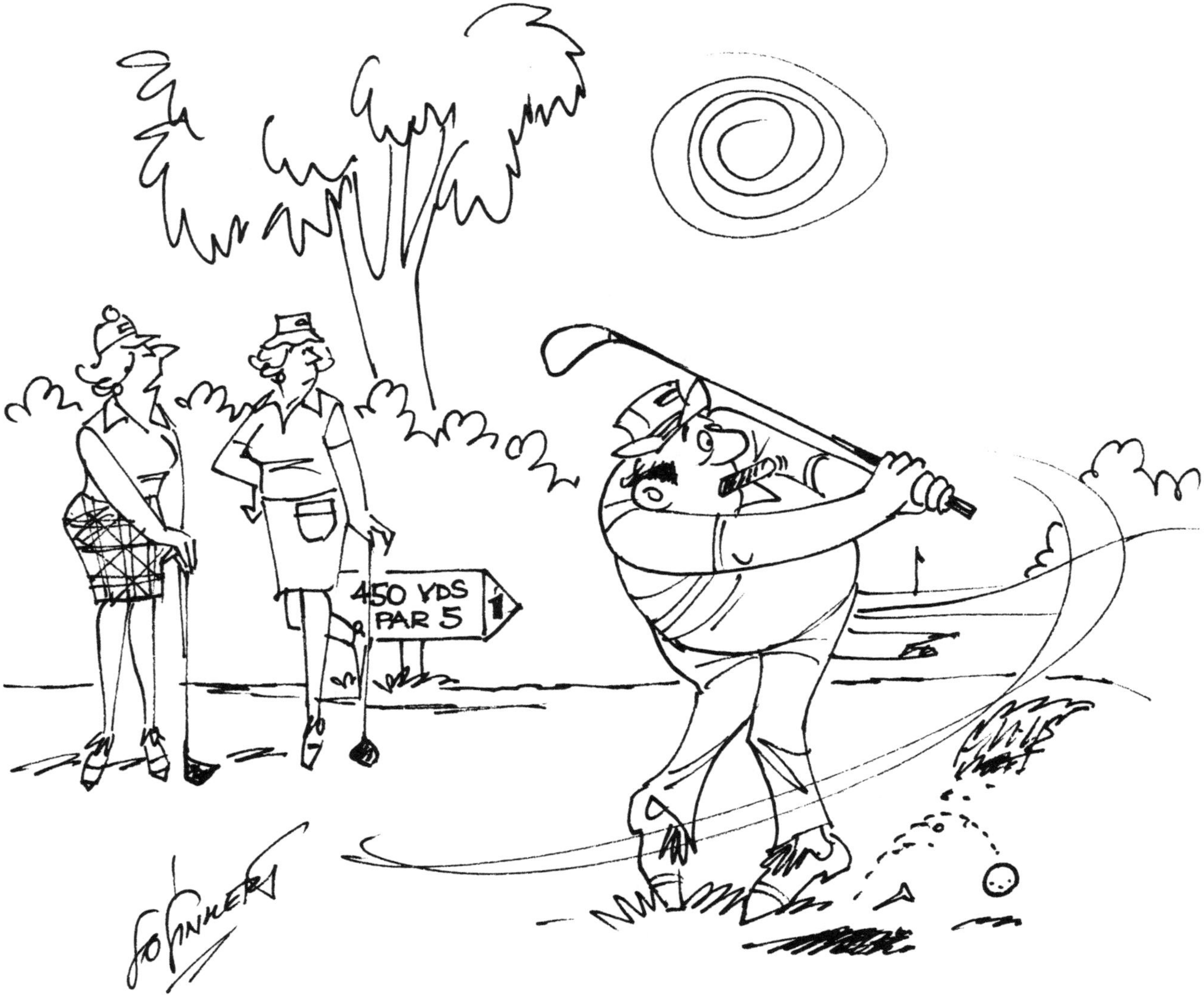
450 YDS
PAR 5
1

"... AND JUST THINK, I MARRIED HIM FOR BEING SUCH A SWINGER."

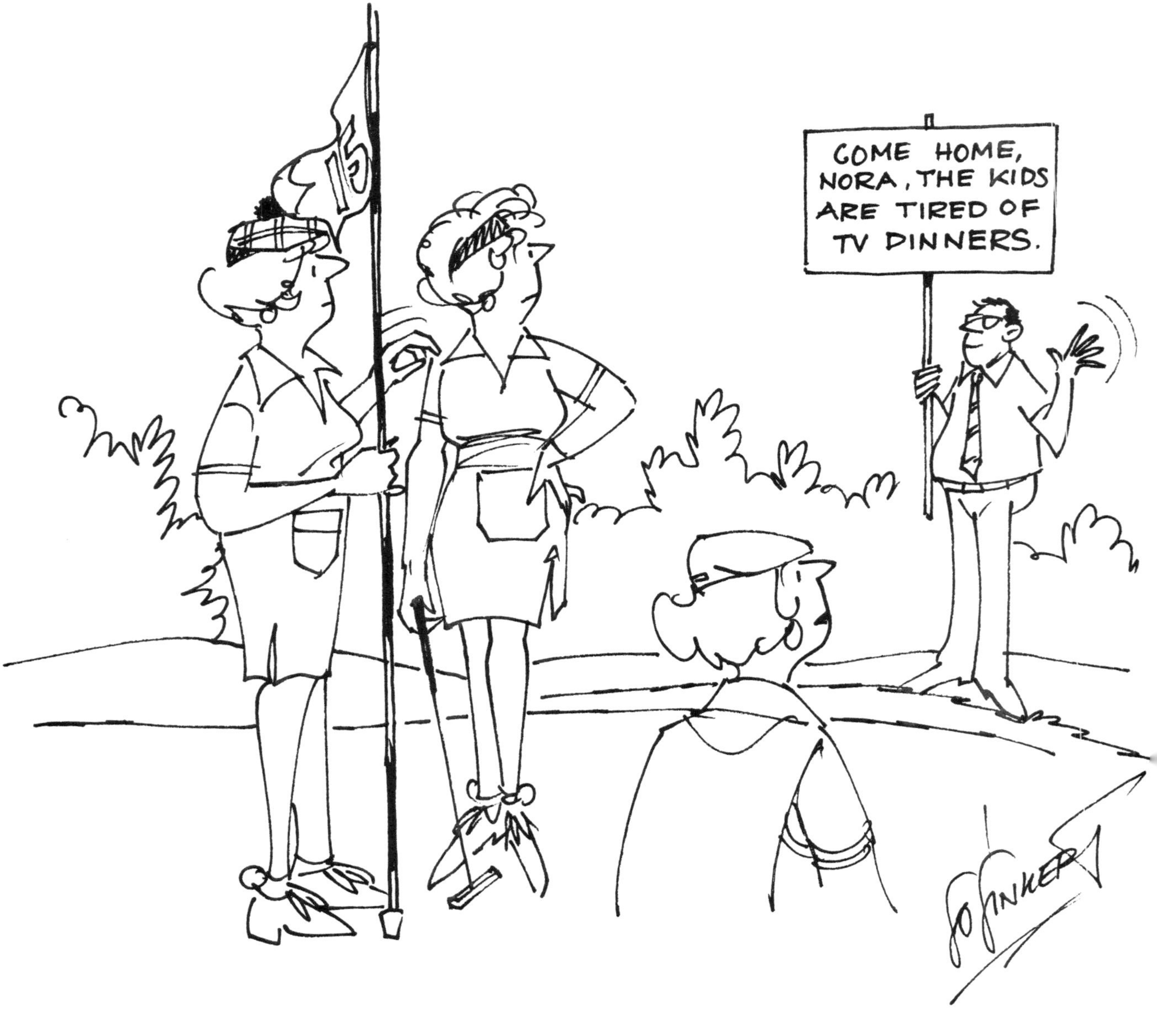
COME HOME, NORA, THE KIDS ARE TIRED OF TV DINNERS.
15

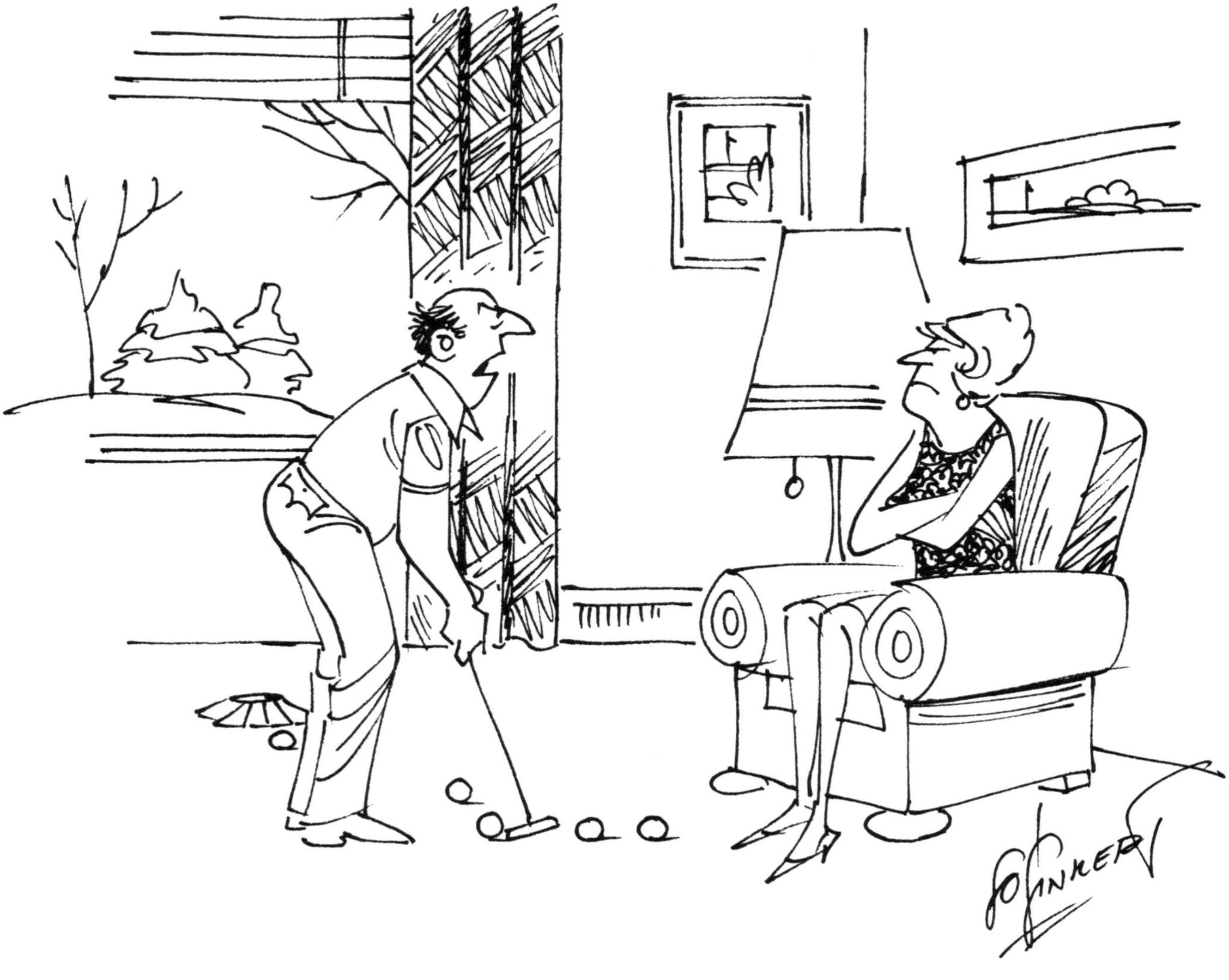

"NO, I'M NOT MARRIED TO GOLF, WE'RE JUST LIVING TOGETHER."

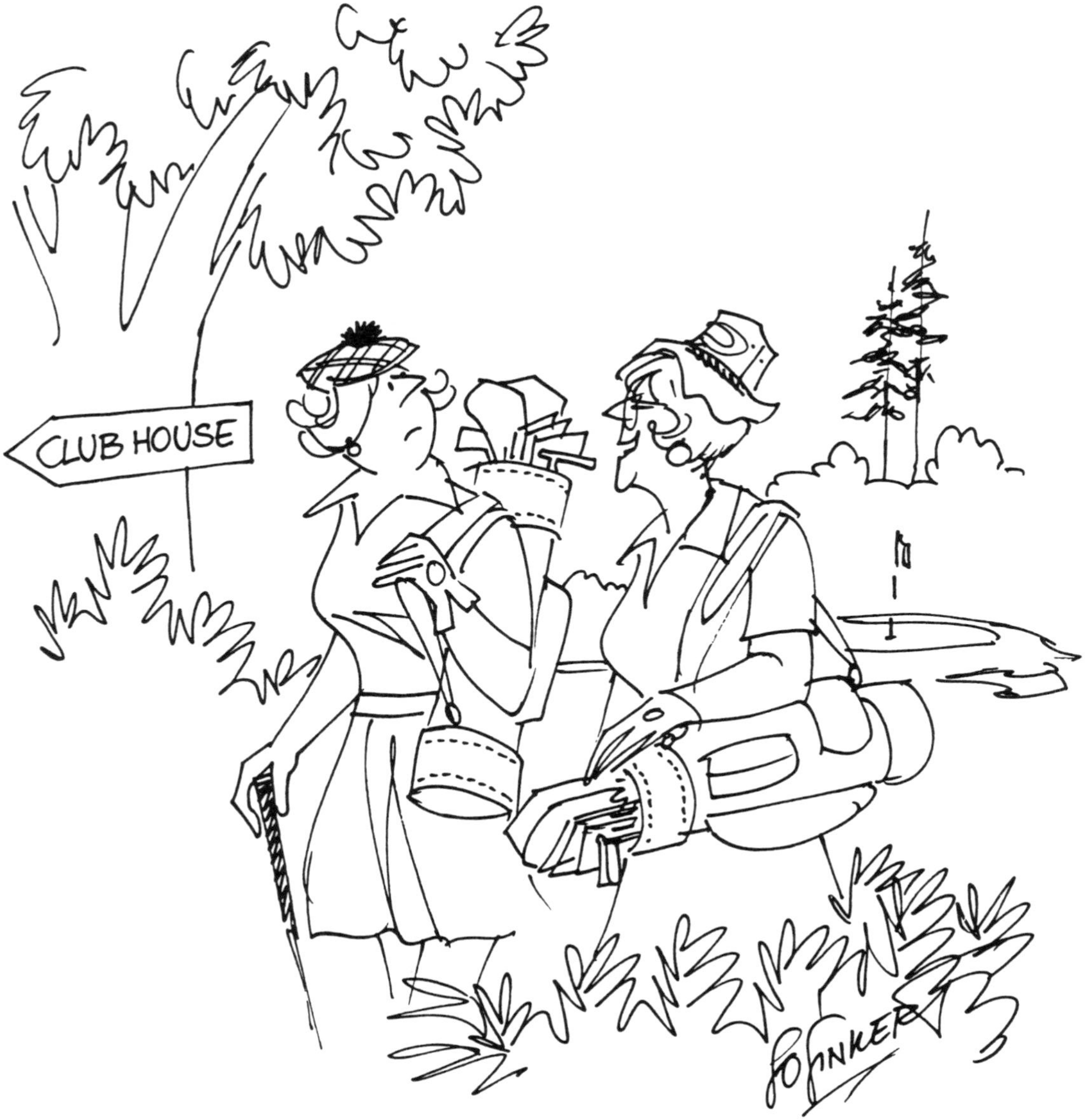
CLUB HOUSE
PINKER

"WELL, I'M GLAD MY FIRST EIGHTEEN HOLES IS OVER; I HATED BEING A BEGINNER."

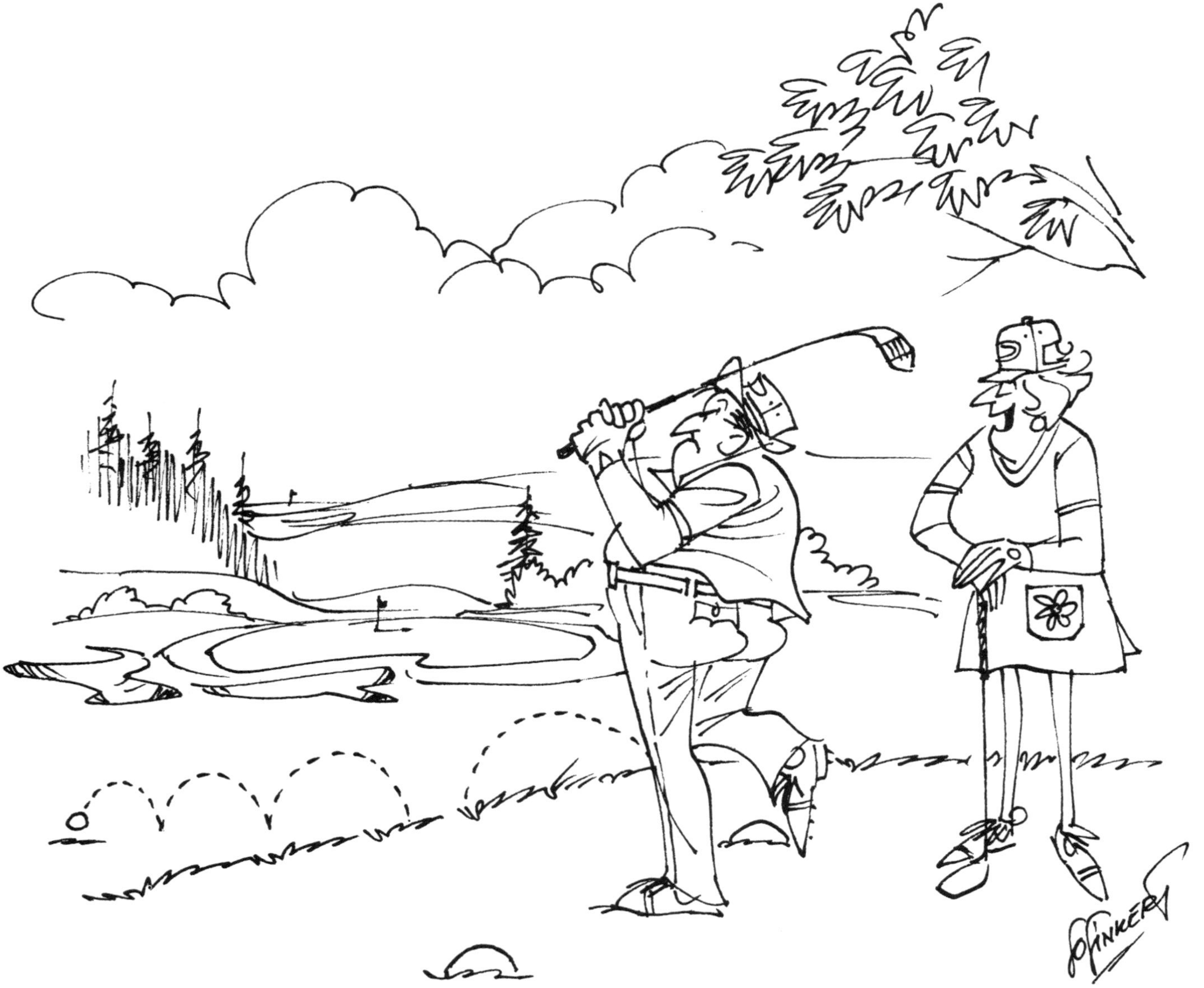

" LOOK AT IT FROM THE POSITIVE SIDE, HONEY, IF IT WAS FOOTBALL IT WOULD'VE BEEN A FIRST DOWN!"

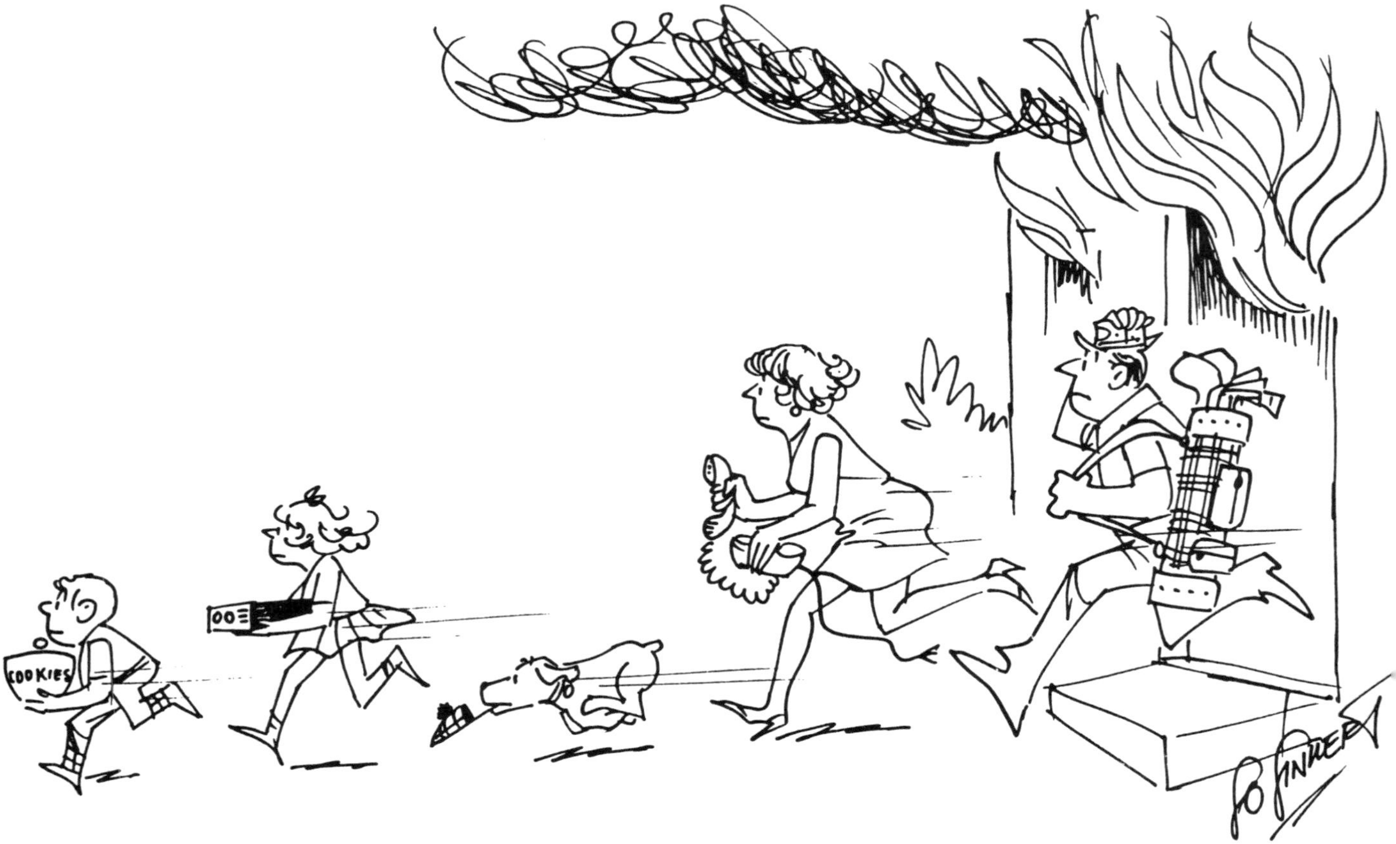
COOKIES

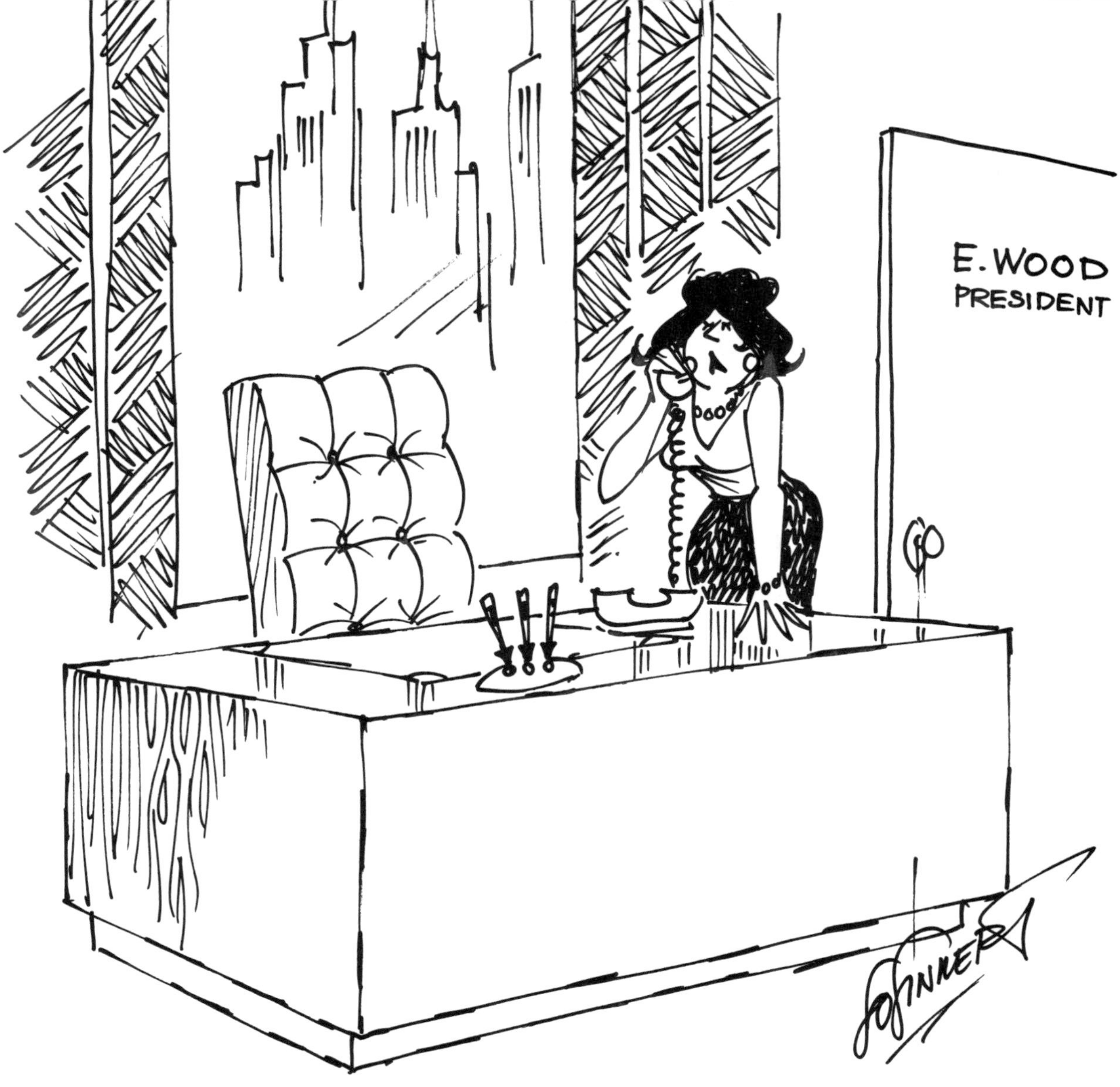
E. WOOD
PRESIDENT

"SORRY, HE'S NOT IN; -- NO, SORRY I'M NOT ALLOWED TO SAY, BUT I'LL GIVE YOU A HINT, IT HAS 18 HOLES AND HE'S NEVER BROKEN A HUNDRED ON IT."

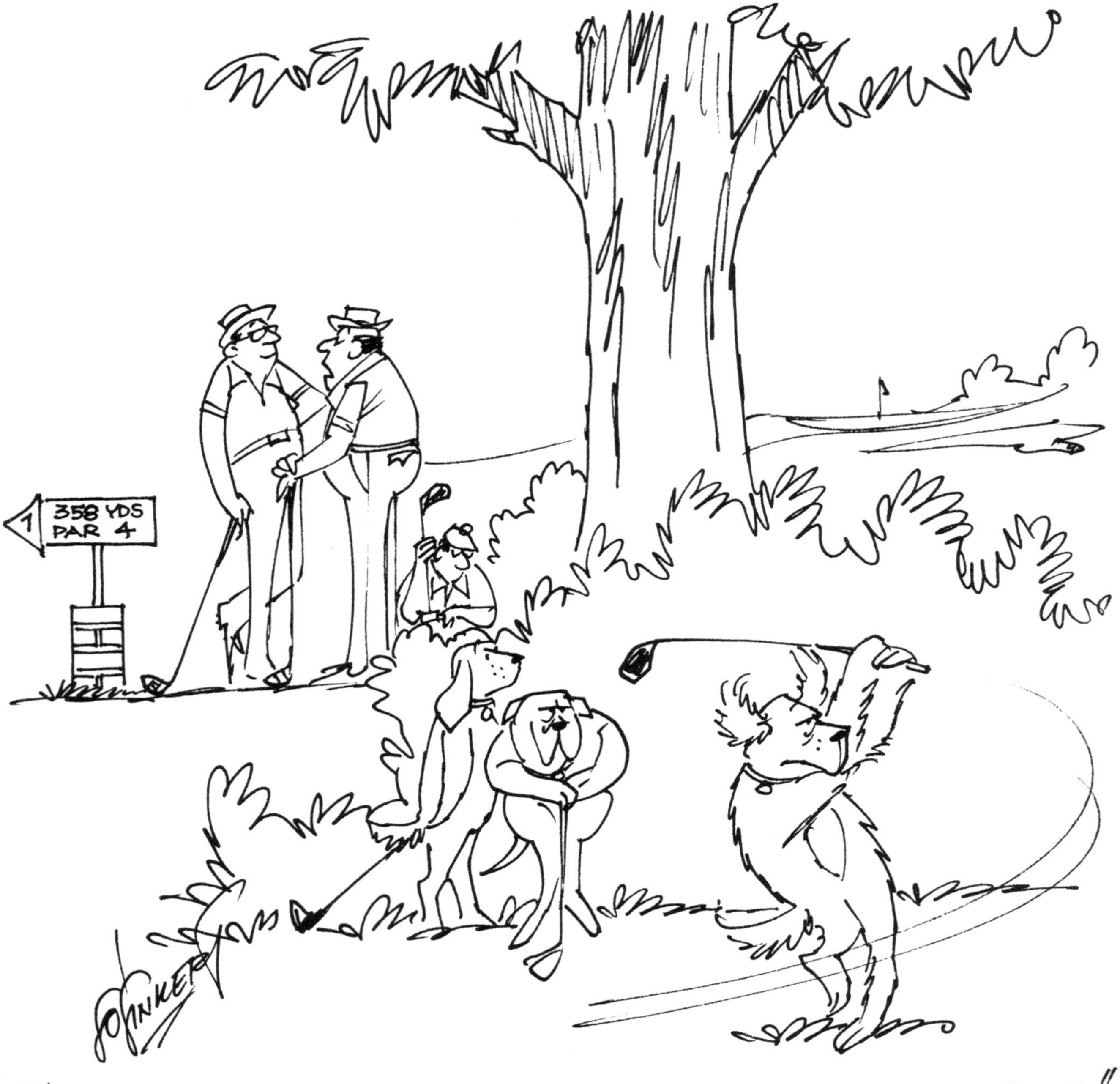
1
358 YDS
PAR 4
PINKER
"EVERYBODY AND HIS DOG TAKES UP THE GAME OF GOLF."

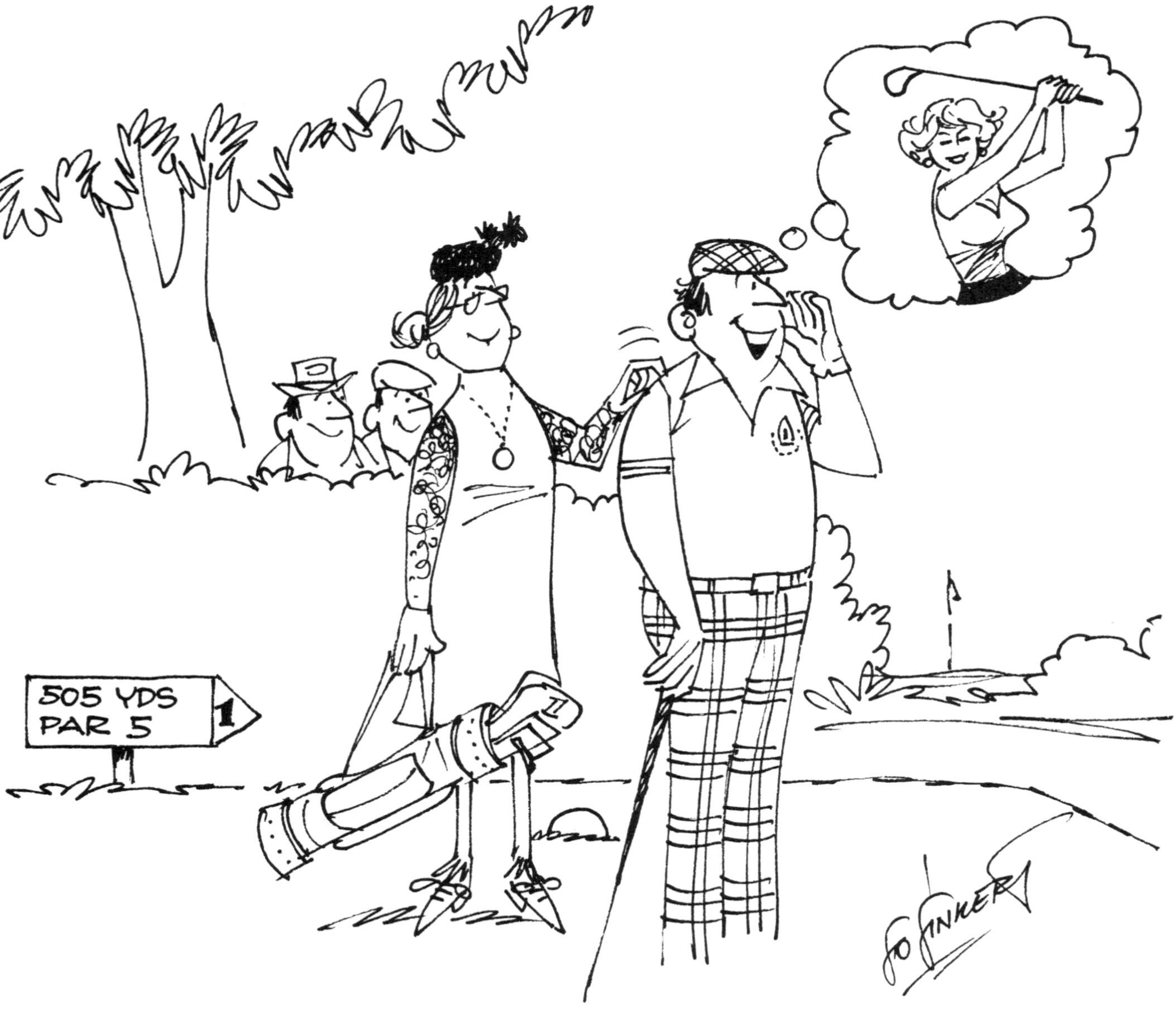
505 YDS
PAR 5
1
JO FINKER

"MISS SCHULZ TO THE TEE PLEASE, YOU'RE MY PARTNER."

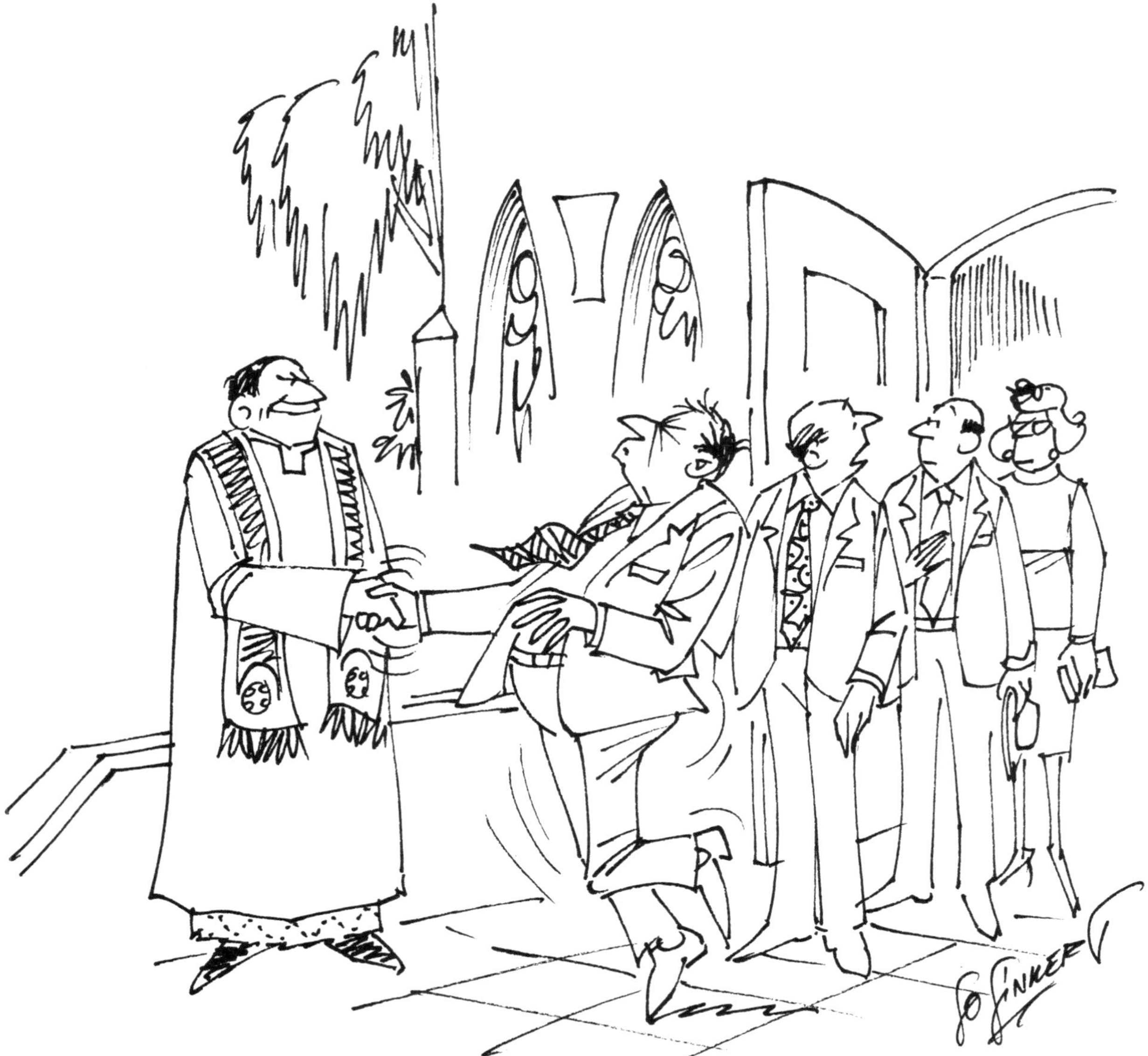

So Sinkert

"WATCH OUT FOR THE REVEREND'S HANDSHAKE, HE CAN RUIN YOUR WHOLE GOLF SEASON!"

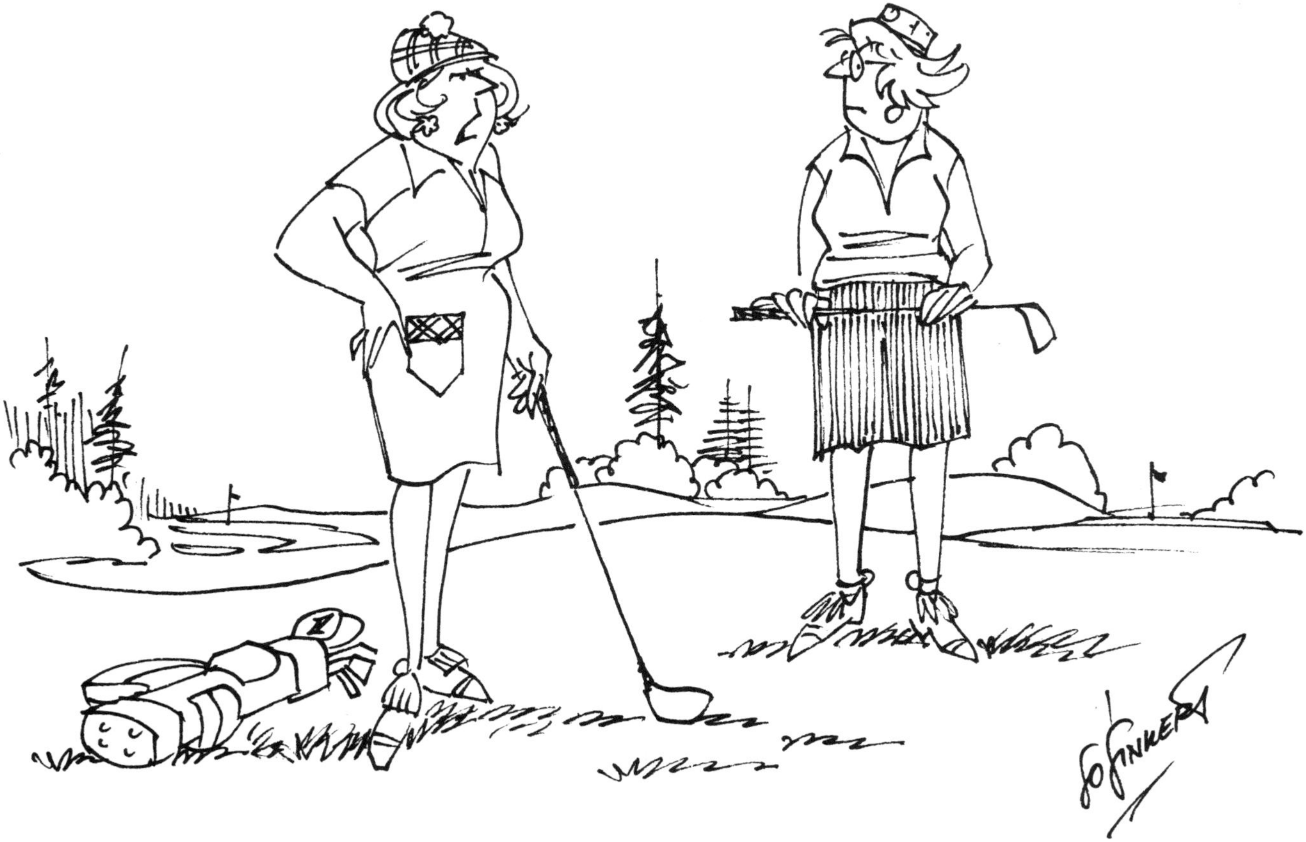
JO FINKERT

"I USED TO ENJOY THE GAME WHEN I HAD NO INTEREST IN IT, THEN I BEGAN TO LIKE IT AND NOW I HATE IT!"

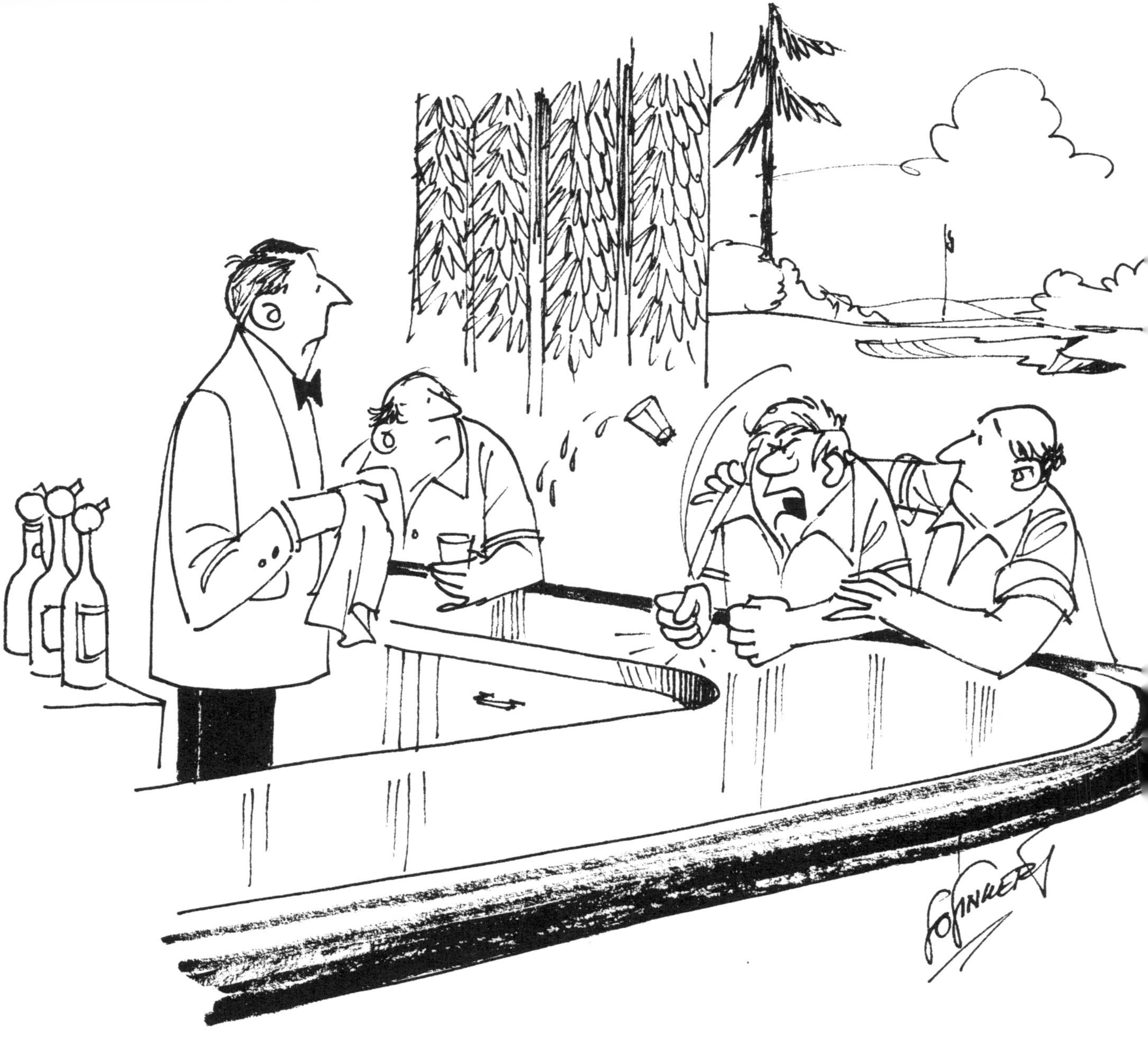
Grinker

"THERE IS SOMETHING WRONG WITH MY GAME WHEN I MISS ALL MY GIMMIES."

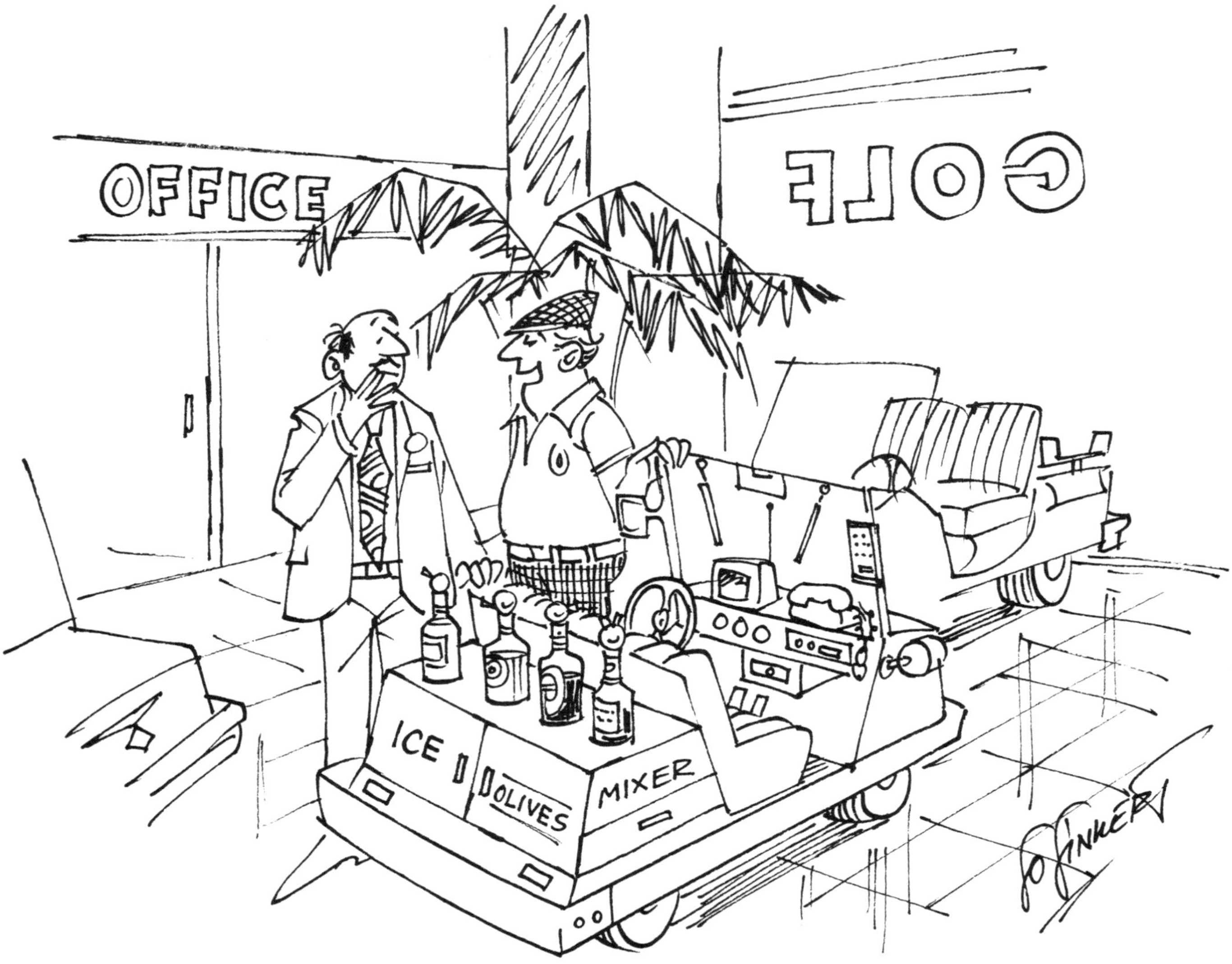
OFFICE
GOLF
ICE
OLIVES
MIXER

"I LOVE THIS BABY, BUT WHERE DO THE GOLF CLUBS GO?"

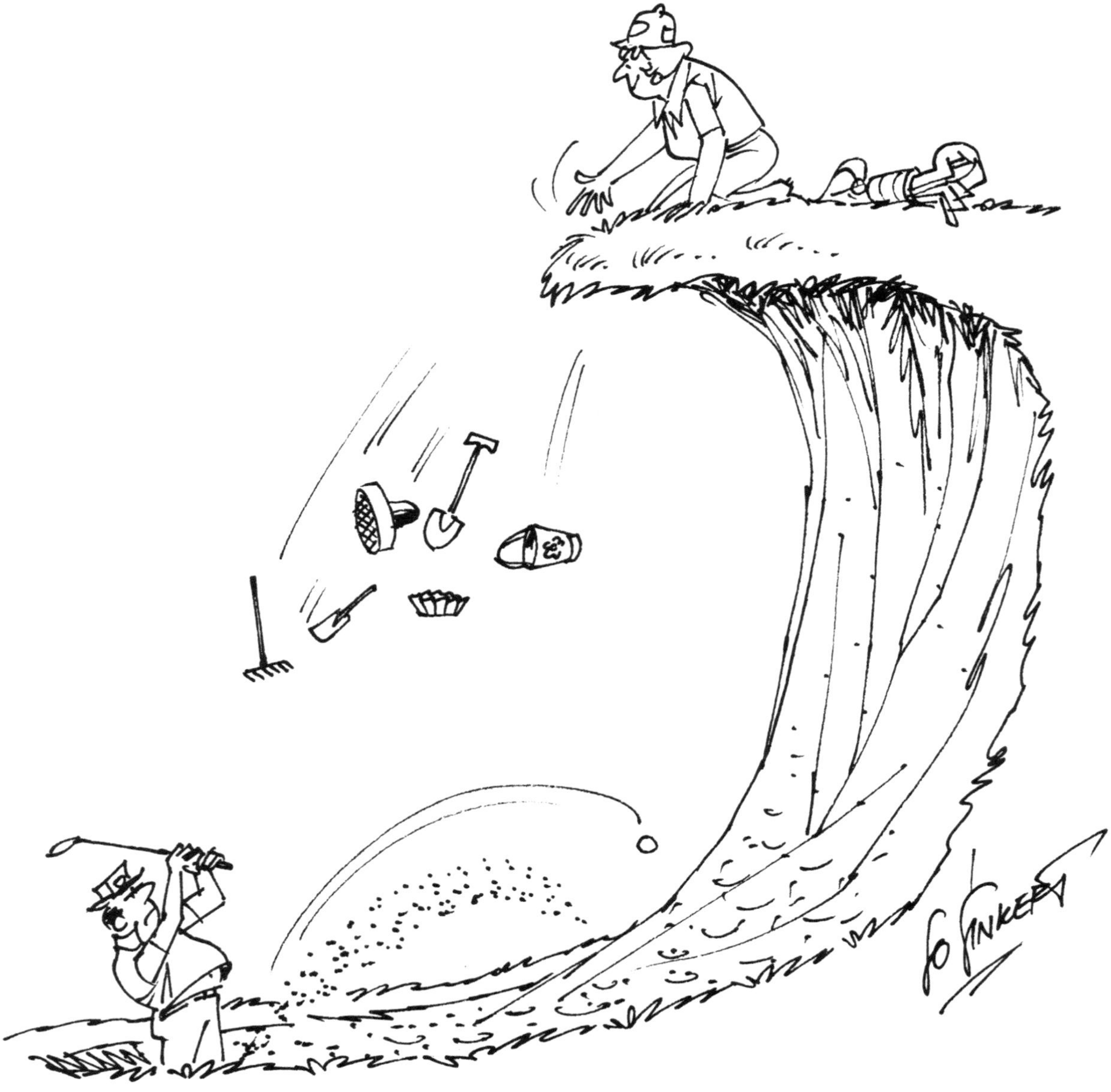

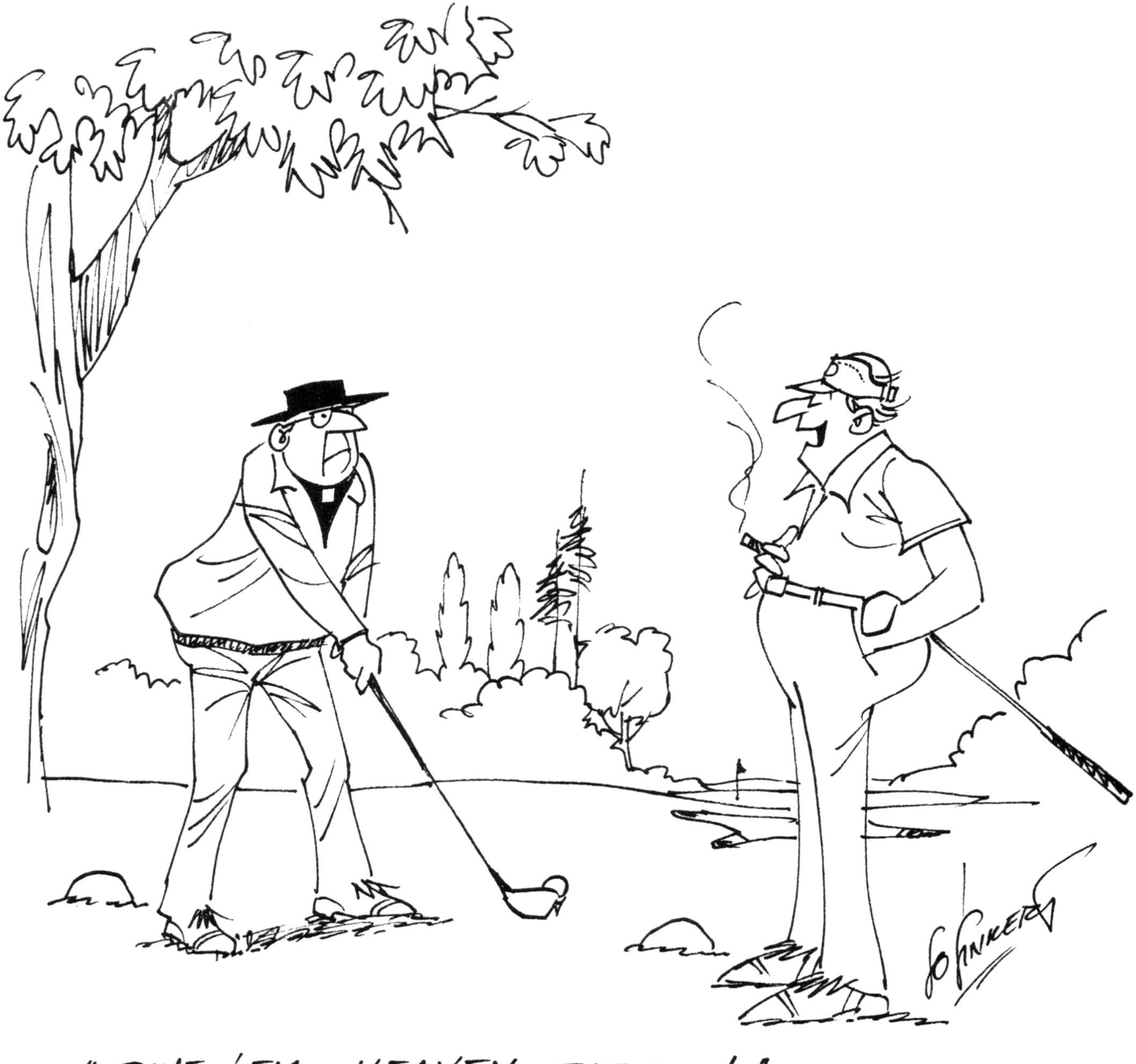

"GIVE 'EM HEAVEN, FATHER!"

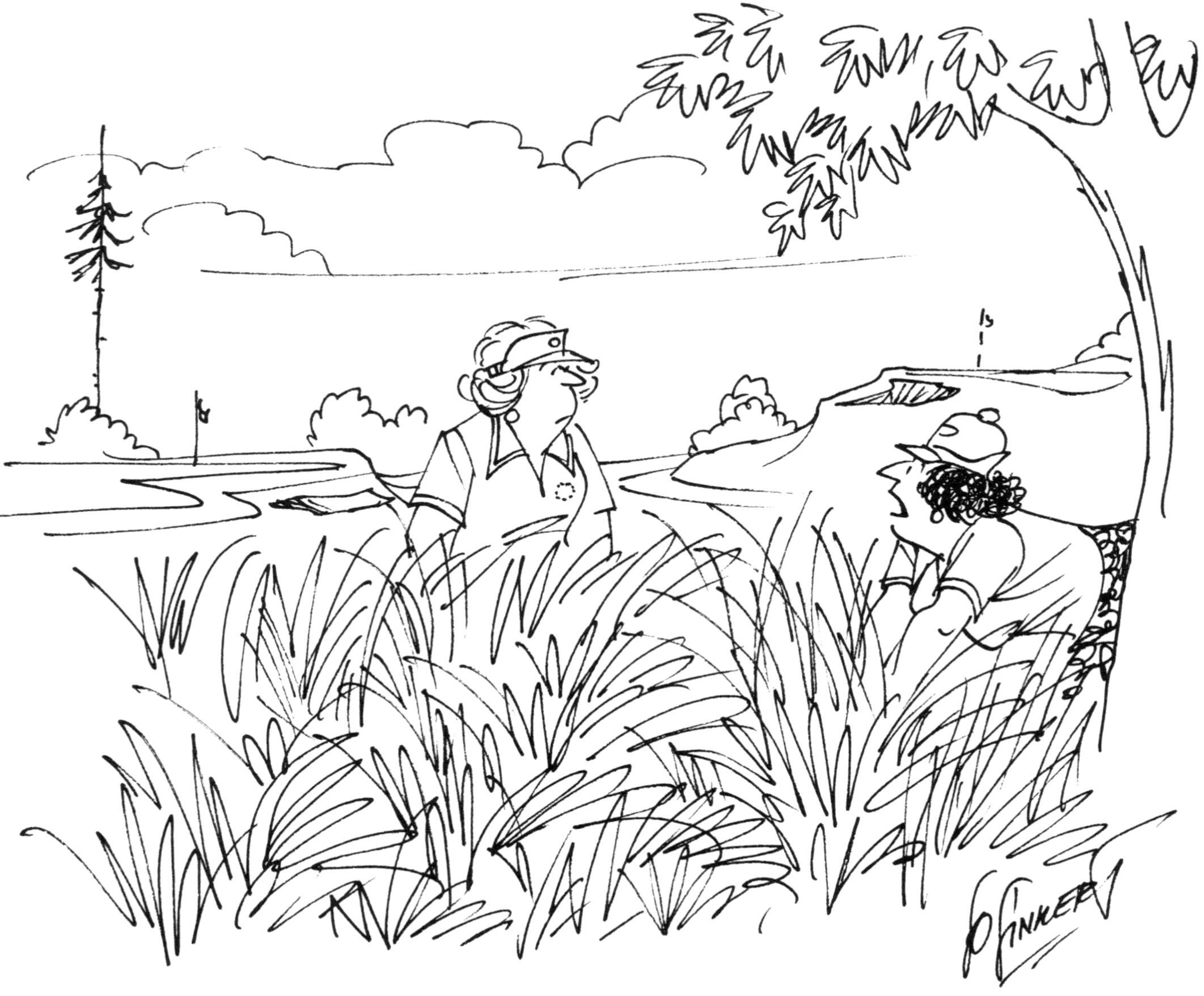

" NEVER MIND ABOUT MY BALL, MARGE...NOW I LOST MY CADDIE."

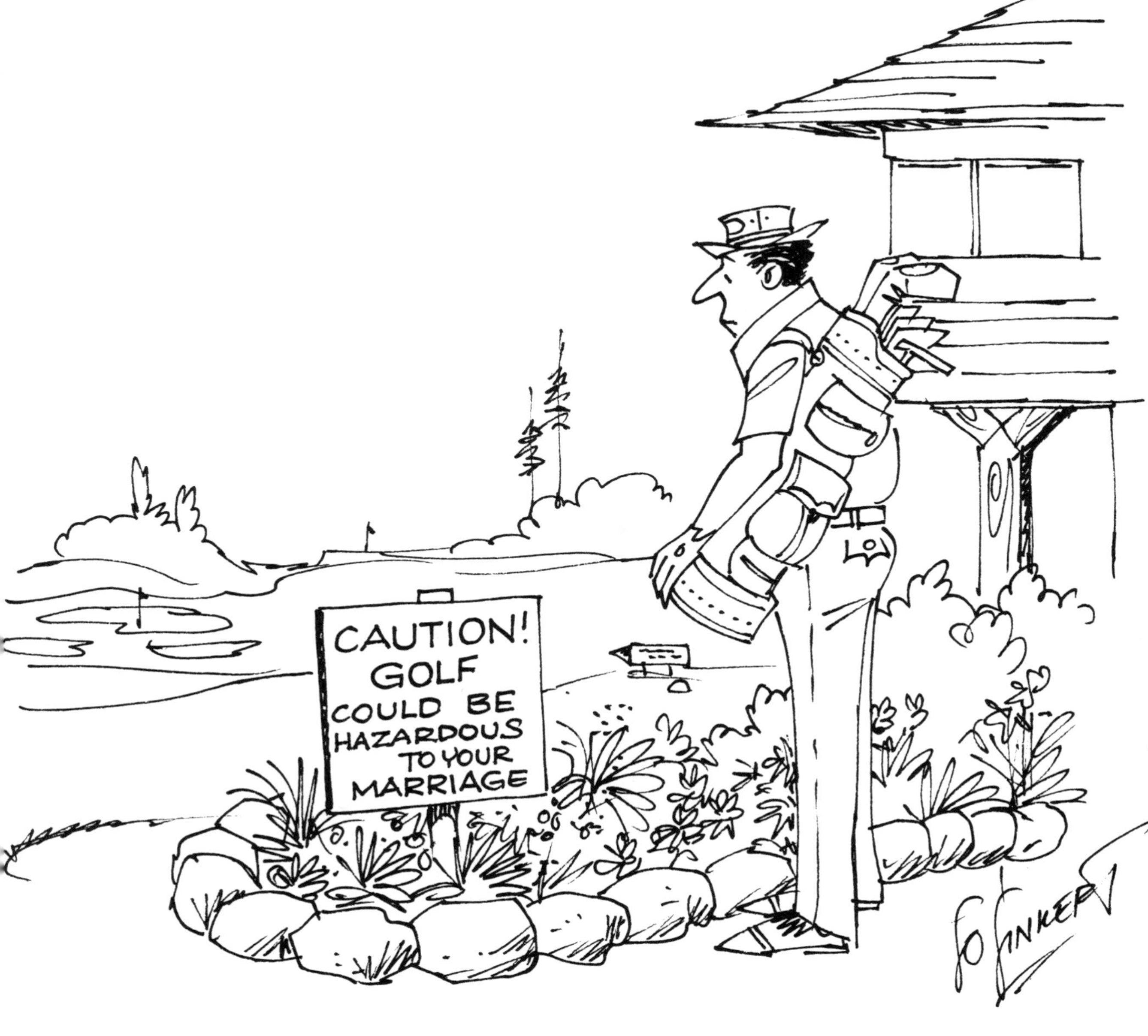
CAUTION!
GOLF
COULD BE
HAZARDOUS
TO YOUR
MARRIAGE

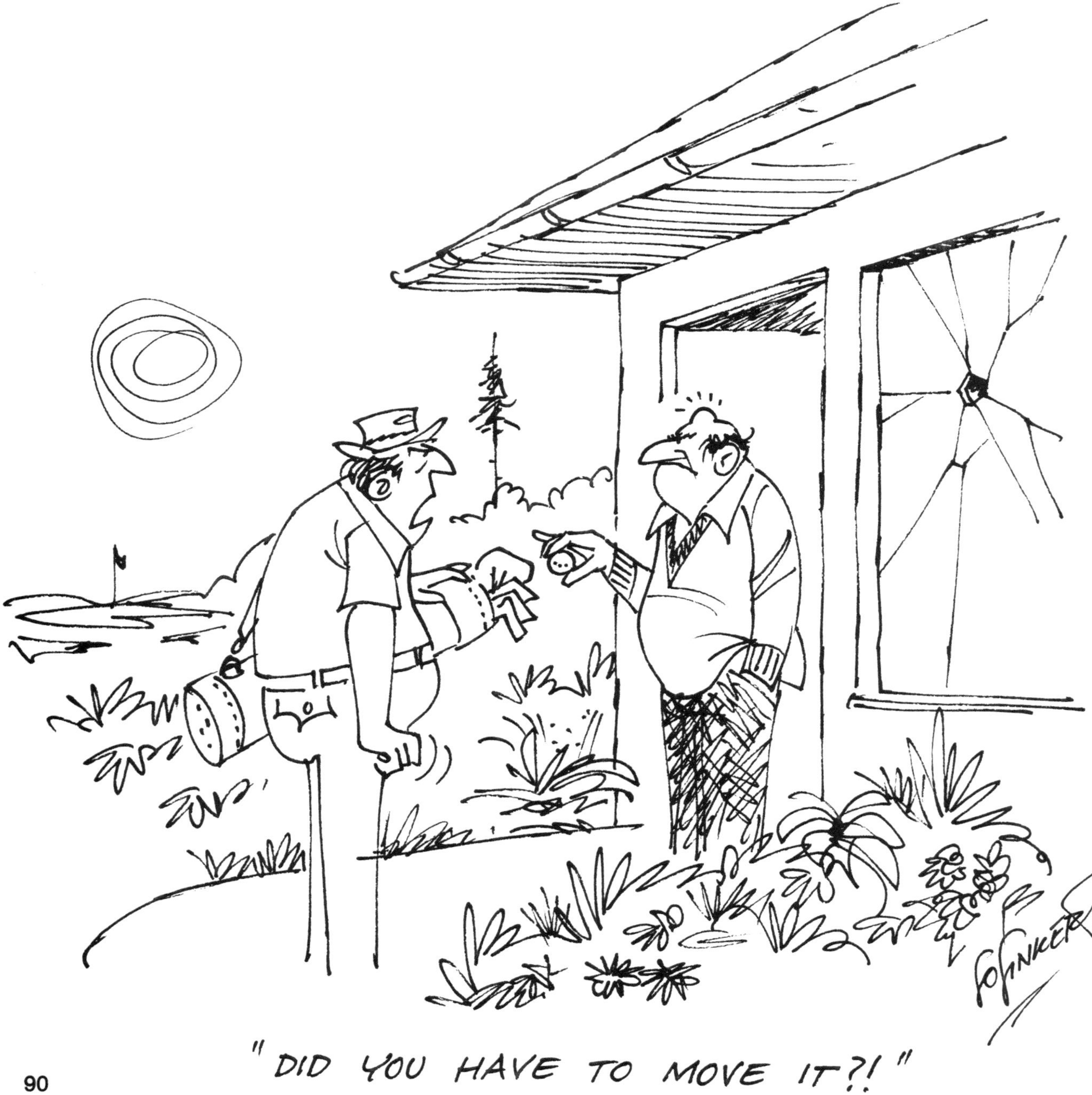

"DID YOU HAVE TO MOVE IT?!"

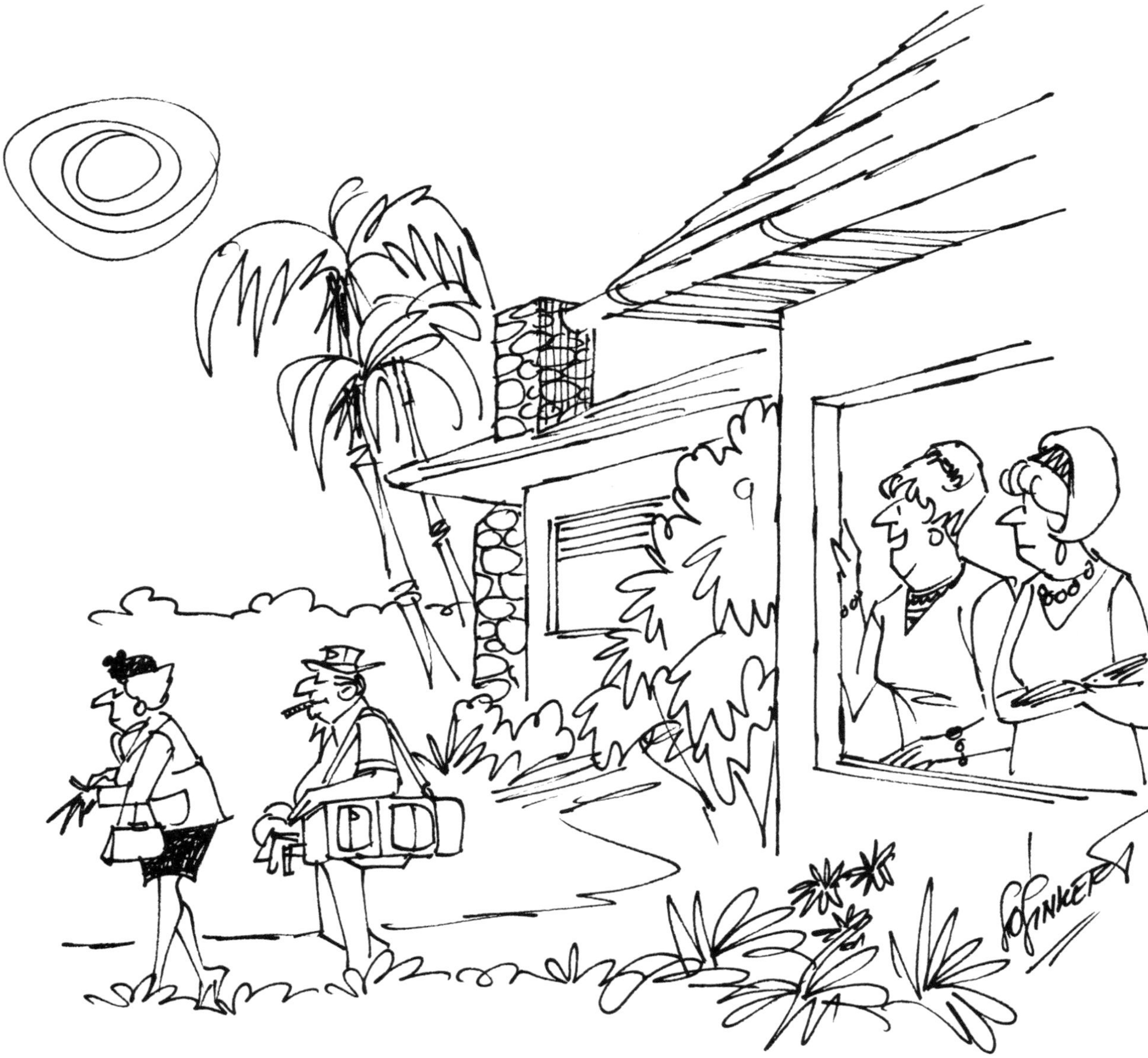

"THAT'S MRS. WESTBURG TAKING HER SPOILED BRAT TO HIS PLAYGROUND."

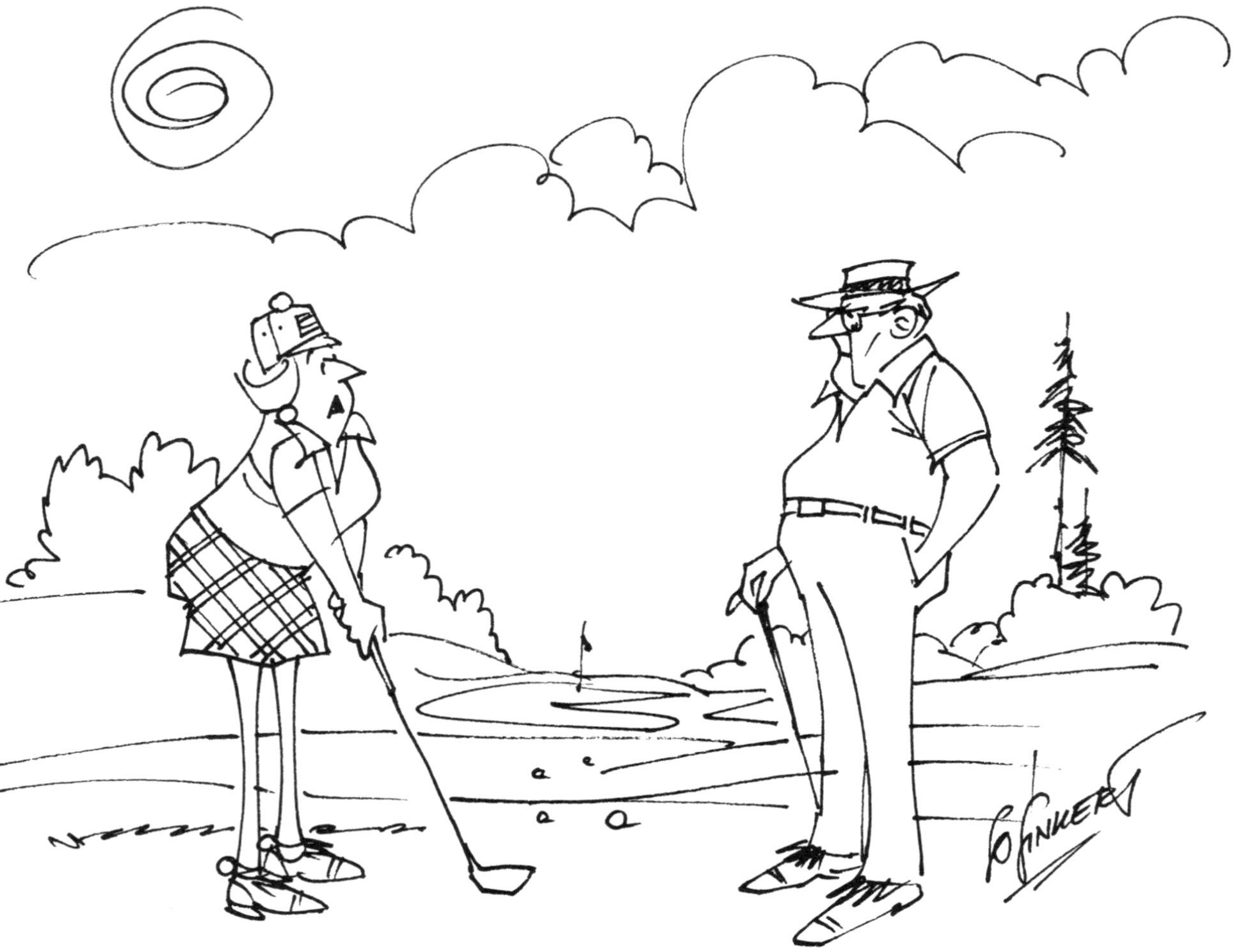

" WELL, ASIDE FROM JERKING MY HEAD, LETTING MY ARM BEND, TOO SMALL A PIVOT, TOO SHORT A BACKSWING AND NO WRIST ACTION...
... HOW DO I LOOK ? "

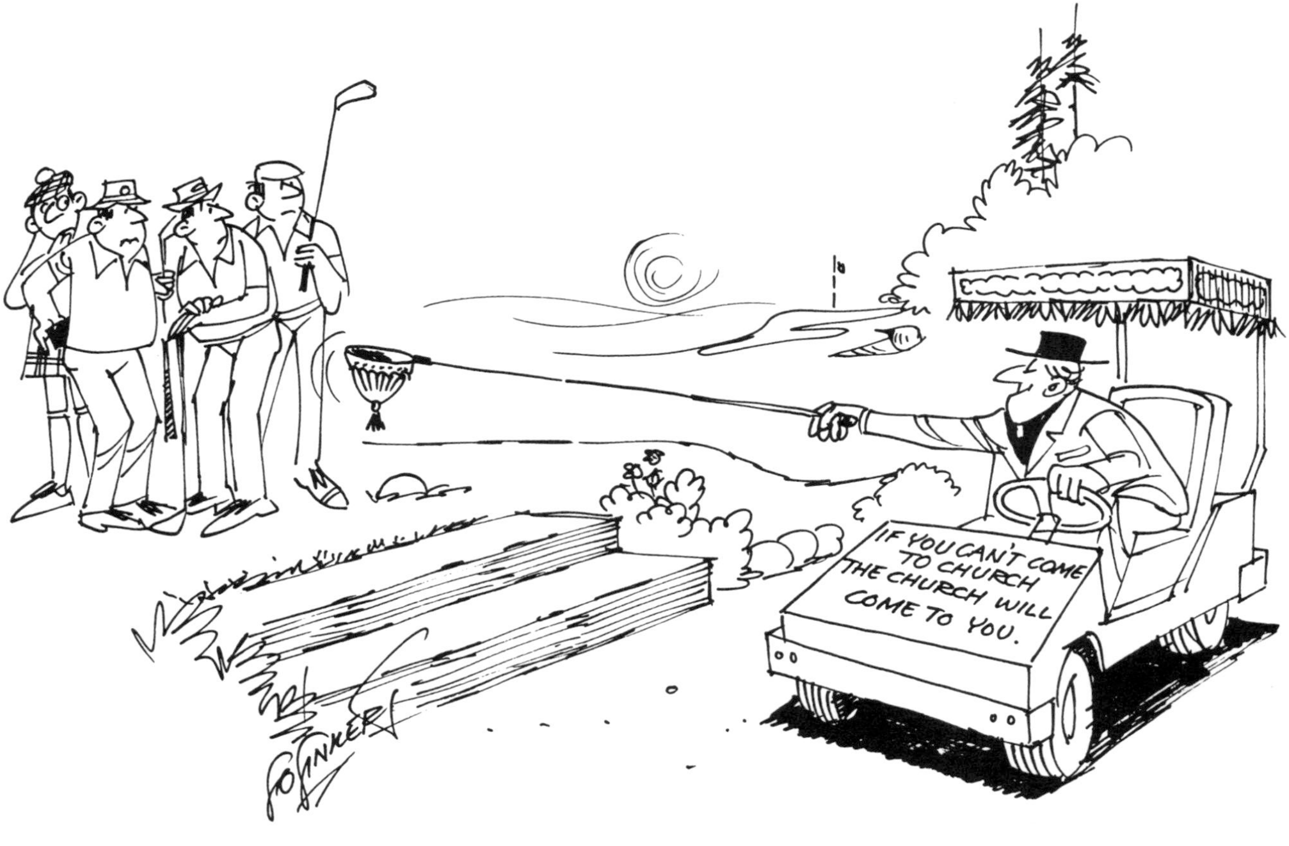
IF YOU CAN'T COME TO CHURCH THE CHURCH WILL COME TO YOU.
GOLDINKER

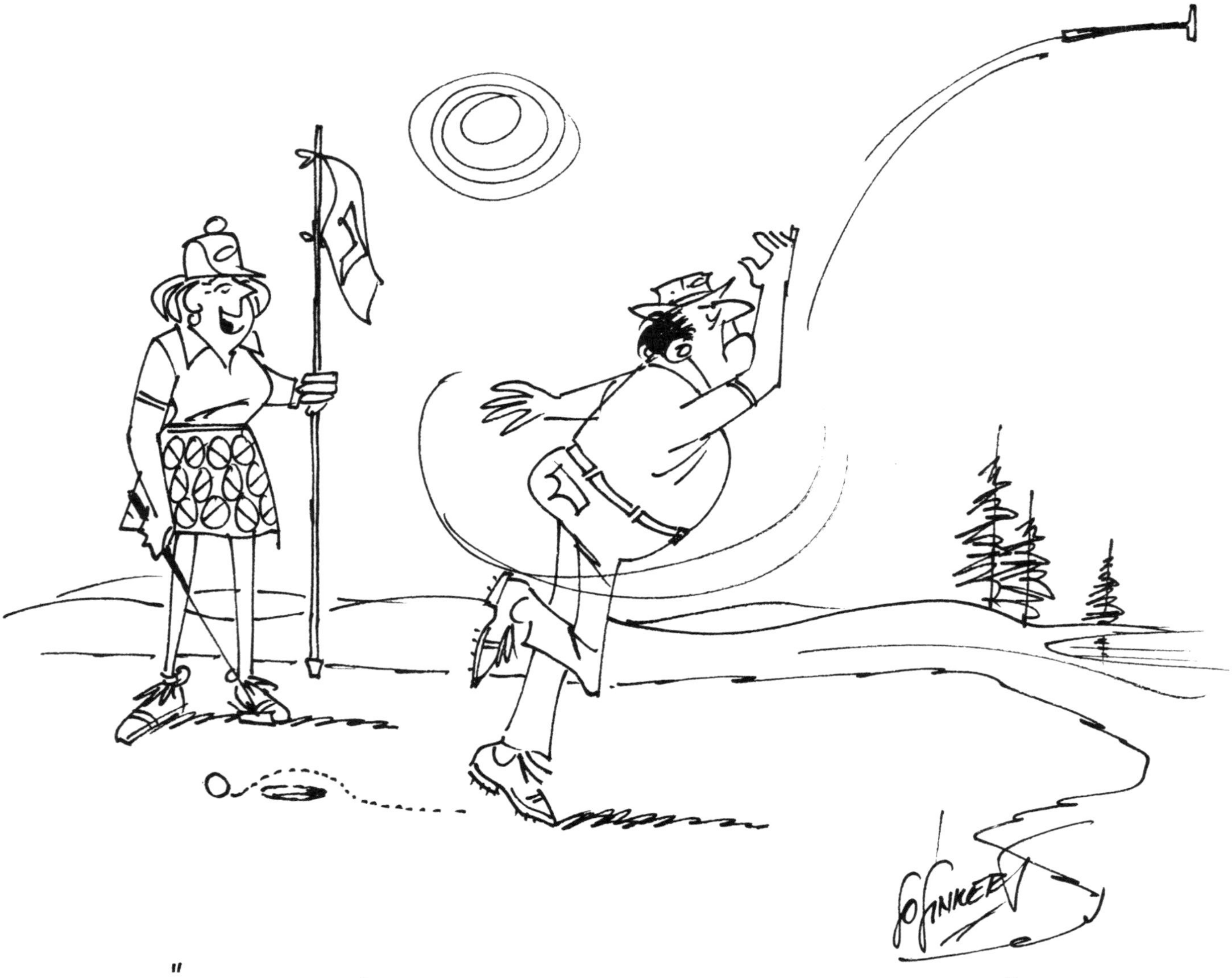

"THERE'S YOUR SLICE AGAIN, HARVEY!"

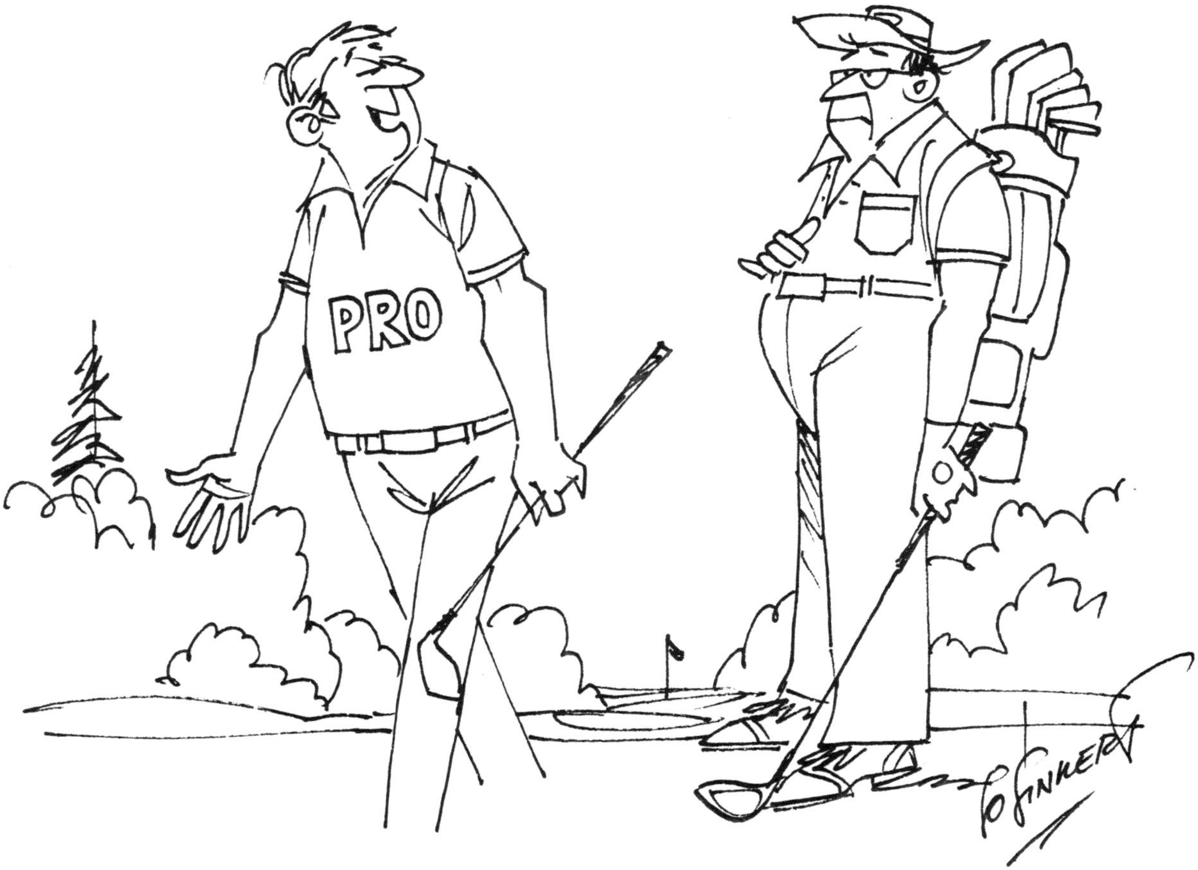
PRO
PINKERT

" WELL DR. REES, YOU HAVE MY OPINION.. PLEASE FEEL FREE TO GET A SECOND OPINION."

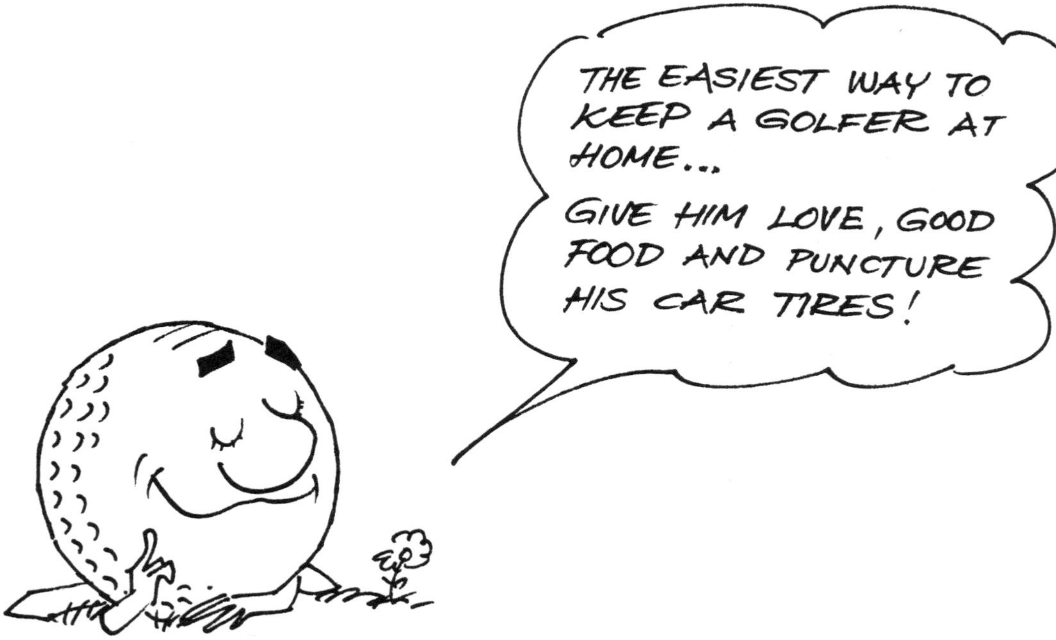
THE EASIEST WAY TO KEEP A GOLFER AT HOME...
GIVE HIM LOVE, GOOD FOOD AND PUNCTURE HIS CAR TIRES!

SPECTACLE LANE PRESS